MOBY FISH

AND

OTHER

WHOPPERS

by RON WATKINS

Printed by Lulu Press, Inc.
Raleigh, NC, USA

Printed in the United States of America

ISBN 978-1-300-37289-9

Thanks -

To my faithful wife who has endured my attempts at humor for 45 years.

To my loving daughter who thinks everything I do is funny.

To my son whom I love to hear laugh. Although he was born on December 21, I am confident that he had nothing to do with the end of the world predicted in the Mayan calendar.

To my son-in-law and daughter-in-law whose dislike for hot apple pie with ice cream on top, which melts down into all the cracks and crevices and tastes delicious, inspired my story of the first Thanksgiving.

To all of my beloved family who inspire me in so many ways and through whom I am able to love and be loved, life's most precious blessing.

To my friend, Jerry, for his diligent proofreading and helpful suggestions.

Finally, to God who helps me see the funny side of life. Since God created laughter, He must have a sense of humor--at least, I certainly hope so when He reads my book.

R. W.

CONTENTS

CONTENTS (Concl.)   PAGE

1 - LET THERE BE LIGHT

In the beginning, God created the heavens and the earth. And the earth was without form and void, and darkness was upon the face of the deep. And God said, "Let there be light!" All of a sudden a light came on and God said, "Ah, good, now I can see better!"

But what God saw saddened Him for the earth was in terrible shape, and God said, "Oy gevalt!" the first time that expression had ever been used. You see, God had previously invented the dinosaurs which were so big and clumsy that they kept bumping into things and making a mess. So God threw a comet at them and they all died.

Then God said, "I need someone to go down there and clean up that mess, someone who will mow the lawns, rake the leaves and bulldoze the dinosaur poop." So He looked in the mirror, liked what He saw and created Man in His own image, out of Silly Putty, and placed him in the Garden of Eden. He named him Eliza Doolittle--oh no, that's another story. He named him Adam, which means *Dirt Ball*, but Adam was no dirt ball. He's the one who named all the plants and animals. For centuries, one question which has puzzled the sages is, "Where did we get the word, *hominy*?" Well, we got it from Adam. One day, God said, "Eliza...I mean Adam, I want you to name all these vegetables. There are 1,000 of them--here's the first one." And Adam said, "Ha many?!"

After a while, Adam was bored, so God decided to make a helpmate for him, someone to do the cooking, the cleaning and the laundry. So God made a woman, which wasn't as easy as it sounds because God had to use one of Adam's ribs to do it. Adam was very ticklish, and every time God tried to take the rib, Adam would start giggling, so God had to knock him out and take the rib when he wasn't looking.

After God created woman, whom He named Eve because He made her at night, He told Adam and Eve to be fruitful and multiply, so they immediately learned their times tables all the way up to ninesies. They weren't too bright at first. Then one morning when they were skinny dipping, Adam looked at Eve and his glasses steamed up because she wasn't wearing any clothes. In fact, they were both naked. To celebrate, they shared an apple. God showed up and said, "Who told you you were naked?" to which Adam replied, "You gotta be kidding!"

Also, God had forbidden them to eat apples because they weren't ripe and He didn't want them getting the green-apple quick step, so He told them to eat only the kumquats.

When He asked them, "Who told you to eat that apple?"

Eve replied, "The snake made me do it."

Adam said, "Eve made me do it."

But she said, "Did not!" and he said, "Did too!"

God said, "What snake?"

This was the first case of passing the buck, and men and women have been arguing ever since.

God decided to punish Adam and Eve by making them have children. Two children they had were Cain and Abel. Cain was jealous of Abel because he was a Boy Scout and could make a better campfire. So one day, Cain bopped Abel on the head with the jawbone of an ass. God didn't like this very much, and neither did the ass, so God banished Cain to the land of Nod near Winken and Blinken. Cain couldn't find it, so he went to Coney Island instead. Today, he's a Guess-Your-Weight barker on the midway.

For many weeks now, people have been trying to find the original Garden of Eden. They've looked everywhere but can't find it. They found King Tut's Tomb, the Lost City of Atlantis and the Empire State Building, but they can't find the Garden of Eden. Some people think God hid it in the Bermuda Triangle. If so, we'll never find it 'cause NOBODY'S GOING IN THERE, EVEN ON A BET!

2 - THE FIRST THANKSGIVING

The Pilgrims were a bunch of people who lived in England many years ago, but they didn't like it there. They liked to eat hot apple pie with ice cream on top which melts down into all the cracks and crevices and tastes delicious. However, the evil king insisted that everyone eat their pie cold with no ice cream. He was known as the world's first Communist. The Pilgrims had heard that Americans honor baseball, hot dogs, APPLE PIE and Chevrolet, so they decided to leave England and fly to America, but the airplane hadn't been invented yet, so they sailed instead.

The first ship they sailed on was the Titanic, but the driver of the ship ran it into Plymouth Rock so hard that it sank (the Titanic, not Plymouth Rock). So they tried again, this time on the H.M.S. Bounty, but the captain was always yelling at the Christians, so they threw him overboard and sailed away to Pit Beef Island where they were never heard from again.

Finally, a third group of Pilgrims selected the Mayflower, but on the way over it broke and had to be repaired using a giant screw. No one remembered to bring a giant screw driver, so they had to use a jack out of the captain's Plymouth. All Pilgrims drove Plymouths because they had heard that Plymouth's "Rock!"

After they landed, the Pilgrims were hungry but had forgotten to bring their lunch, so the Indian Chief, Minnehaha, sent some Indians to help them: Squanto, Tonto and Bob Feller. The Indians brought corn which they called *maize* because they were always getting lost in the corn field. That's why today a place where people get lost is called a *maze*. The Pilgrims didn't like the maize though because the Indians fertilized it with fish, causing John Alden to remark to Priscilla Baumgartner, "Speaking for myself, this corn tastes like fish." Everyone agreed, so they all went out to get something else to eat.

At first, they tried pigeons and sea gulls, but there wasn't enough meat on them. They needed something larger, so Steve Irwin said they should try ostriches, but there weren't enough ostriches in America at that time. Benjamin Franklin suggested they try turkey since it was a native American bird, and he owned a turkey farm. Everyone liked the turkey, and they all wanted drumsticks, but there weren't enough to go around. In an effort to satisfy everyone, Ben invented a turkey with six legs, but it took off running and they weren't able to catch the stupid thing!

So the next thing they did was to cross a turkey with an octopus producing enough drumsticks for everybody, but some people thought it tasted like fish. Also, whenever the turkeys saw a turkey hunter coming, they would say, "Baa," and the hunters wouldn't shoot them because they thought they were sheep. So the Pilgrims ended up going to Super Fresh to buy all their turkeys, and it was cheaper than buying them from Benjamin Franklin.

After they had bought enough turkeys, Abraham Lincoln threw a big feast which he called *Thanksgiving*. He invited all the Indians over, and everyone enjoyed turkey, maize and hot apple pie with ice cream on top which melts down into all the cracks and crevices and tastes delicious. They also played their favorite music, Plymouth Rock, featuring Bruce Bedspring. Tonto brought his faithful friend, Kemosabe, but he wasn't allowed to stay because he was wearing a mask, and nobody trusted him. He would later become famous for riding a white horse, yelling "Hi-yo Silver," and shooting silver bullets at people.

So this Thanksgiving, as you're enjoying your turkey, maize and hot apple pie with ice cream on top which melts down into all the cracks and crevices and tastes delicious, be thankful for the Pilgrims, turkeys, maize, Minnehaha, Benjamin Franklin and Abraham Lincoln. Also be thankful that you're not a turkey. And don't forget the hot apple pie with...

14

3 – THE FOURTH OF JULY

The Fourth of July is a national holiday that we celebrate every July 4th, also known as Arbor Day. A long time ago, we got tired of the way England was treating us so we asked Jefferson Davis to write a Declaration of Independence. Its opening words are forever emblazoned on the minds of every American: "Four score and seven years ago..." In fact, they became so famous that Abraham Lincoln used them as his address when he lived in Gettysburg.

One of the things we didn't like was the Stamp Act. The price of a stamp back then was only 3 cents, but the King of England and Parliament wanted to raise it to $54.40. So we told them to shove it. Parliament was always causing trouble. Even in England some people didn't like it, and one guy named Fawkes tried to blow it up. Now, every year, they celebrate Guy Fawkes Day by blowing up Parliament.

Another thing was the price of tea, so a bunch of mischievous colonials, including Davy, Davy Crockett, Daniel Boone and his brother Pat, Joe DiMaggio and Juan Valdez, thought it would be fun to dress up as Indians and have a tea party. But the tea tasted like coffee, so they dumped it all in the harbor. Today, this event is known as the Whiskey Rebellion. Well, England didn't like this so they sent troops over to live with the colonists and keep an eye on them. This only made people angrier, and they kept telling the soldiers to get out, but they wouldn't listen. So the colonists passed a second amendment to the Constitution that says, "Every free man is entitled to bear a gun and shoot anybody that comes to his house."

The two opposing factions were represented by the Hatfields and the Tories, today known as Democrats and that other party. The leader of the Tories was Victor Tory. He would later become famous for acting in *Gone With the Wind* as the overseer and getting dirt thrown in his face. If he had read the book, he would have known that was going to happen.

An initial encounter occurred between the British regulars and the American Minutemen, so named by their wives, at Lexington, MA, where they exchanged gunfire in what became known as, *The shot heard around the world!* As far away as Glen Burnie, somebody said, "What was that?" and was told, "That was the shot heard around the world." Patrick Henry stood up and said, "Give me liberty, or give me death!" so they gave him death and that shut him up. Then the king sent over all his ships and submarines and everybody went to war.

The war lasted for a hundred years, so they cleverly named it The Hundred Years War, one of the longest on record. It became a family tradition and was passed down from father to son. Even England and France never fought that long, and they were always fighting. The French didn't like the English because they called the English Channel the English Channel, and the French said, "It's not yours." They also were disgusted with the English because they eat pies made with kidneys, and the English said, "Well, you eat snails! Yuck!" This debate continues today. The English also didn't like the French because they talked funny and still do even after all the fighting. Maybe their underwear's too tight.

Americans should really appreciate the French because without their help, we would have won the war much quicker. They also sent us the Eiffel Tower and Mt. Rushmore. The war finally came to an end soon after the battle of Yorktown in which the French were very instrumental. They all brought their instruments and played a lot of French music while the Americans and British held their ears. One piece they played that the soldiers liked was the minuet, but it's very hard to dance while wearing combat boots.

General Cornswaggle was there leading the British, while George Washington led the American troops. The French were led by the Marquis de Lafayette de la Sal which means "Get me Salma Hayek's phone number." General Washington called him *Froggy* for short because he was only five four, and Washington didn't know his first name. General Cornswaggle called him other names.

The Americans so valued the French assistance during the war, that when World War I started, American General John Pershing went to France and said, "Well, Lafayette, here we are," to which the French replied, "It's about time, the Revolution ended 130 years ago! And who's Lafayette?"

The American people were so happy the war was over that they all wanted to make George Washington President of the United States. He said, "Okay, but only if you put my picture on the dollar bill and the quarter," to which they readily agreed, except for a few left over Tories who just wanted to get even by throwing dirt in his face.

And the rest is history.

4 - A TRIP TO PHILADELPHIA

I know, I know, as soon as someone mentions going to Philadelphia, some clown will step forward and say something like, "Duh, I spent two weeks in Philadelphia one day. Har! Har! Har!" and then laugh so hard that his big red nose falls off. Well, I'm here to tell you to stop it! It is irreverent and disrespectful to make jokes about our nation's capital, no matter how funny they are. My trip to Philly was just fine, thank you.

Philly is a nickname someone gave the city. It's named after the Philly Cheese Steak sandwich which is a Philadelphia delicacy. You haven't been there unless you've had a Philly Cheese Steak. It was invented by Benjamin Franklin. Some people told him he should name it the Benjy Cheese Steak, but he said, "No, just having my picture on the three dollar bill is enough." He was a very humble man.

One of your first stops when you visit Philly, is the new Visitor's Center in the old historic district. It was built by Benjamin Franklin. In it, you will find an information desk and a bathroom. I don't know how they use the other 800,000 square feet. In the bathroom is a very powerful machine which blows your hands dry in just 12 seconds. I'm thinking they should make one of these big enough for the whole body. Just think of the laundry bills you would save from not having to wash all those towels, not to mention the thrill of drying off.

The information desk is a lot of fun. They will go to no lengths to answer your questions, and if they can't answer them, they'll give you a map of the city. I entertained them by asking questions about the meaning of life and Salma Hayek's phone number. I got a lot of maps that day.

To get rid of you, they will schedule you for one of the tours of Independence Hall which run every minute and a half all day long. It was originally called the State House, as smugly pointed out by our tour guide. Don't you hate it when those tour guides act like they know so much more than you do?

Ah, Independence Hall, where everybody does what he wants, thus the name. It was here that such great historical documents as The Declaration of Independence, The Constitution of the United States and the Mayflower Compact were written and signed. It is an awesome feeling when you're ushered into the great Assembly Room where such magnificent historical figures as George Washington, Thomas Jefferson, Benjamin Franklin and E. Pluribus Unum actually sat smoking their hookahs, playing Mah Jongg and posing for paintings.

And John Hancock. What can I say about John Hancock? Not much, except that he was a big showoff, writing his name 10 times larger than anyone else when he signed The Emancipation Proclamation. He said it was so the British would have no trouble reading it, but it was actually because he was trying to impress Molly Pitcher who so far wouldn't give him the time of day or a drink of water. Also, he had forgotten his glasses, put his powdered wig on backwards and couldn't see a thing. Franklin offered him a pair of the new bifocals he had just invented, but Hancock said, "Ya gotny more a tha' stuff we were smokin' in the hookahs?" Then they high-fived, and Franklin went off and invented daylight saving time.

Benjamin Franklin invented most of the things we use today. In addition to those things already named, here's a partial list:

The Franklin Stove	The library	The post office
The Franklin Doorknob	The keyhole	The parachute
The Franklin Fly Swatter	The beeper	Electricity
The Franklin Pogo Stick	The sundial	The outhouse
The Franklin Can Opener	Radial tires	The wheel

The list could go on and on. In fact, whenever anyone asks you who invented anything, just say, "Benjamin Franklin," and chances are you'll be right.

He also held many positions in his life-long, political career, including standing, sitting and lying down. He was never very good at standing on one leg, though, because he had the gout which accounted for his surly disposition. He once yelled at Betsy Ross, "Oh, make it red, white and blue for all I care!"

Franklin was also the publisher of *Poor Richard's Almanack* in which he published many of the clever sayings attributed to him, such as, "Early to bed, early to rise makes a man healthy, wealthy and wise." He also said, "You can't see over an elephant without using a stepladder." My favorite of his sayings is, "You can pick your friends and you can pick your nose, but you can't pick your friend's nose." Benjamin Franklin annoyed a lot of people, so when he died he was buried under 10 tons of marble just in case he tried to come back.

Actually, there are some people trying to resurrect him. They have this thing they call, *Breakfast with Benjamin Franklin,* a rather macabre notion. It's something like *Breakfast with Santa Claus,* except Santa's a real person. What they do is get a bunch of people together and invite Franklin to join them for breakfast. I don't think he has shown up yet, but if he ever does, you'll never see a room clear any quicker.

The next thing you're sure to see in Philadelphia is the Liberty Bell. There it is in all its glory, with that big, ugly crack running right up the middle. Seems like they would have fixed it by now, but every time they try, it just gets worse. I wonder if they tried Superglue. When it first cracked, someone said, "Let's just throw it away," but Franklin said, "No, a lot of people will want to see it someday, and we can charge everyone thruppence." Franklin was also very frugal. No one knew what thruppence was but it sounded good so they said okay. Now, of course, there's no charge since they figure no one would pay anything to see an old, cracked bell anyway.

Before you leave Philadelphia, you must stop at the Betsy Ross house, if you can find it. It's a very tiny structure and easy to miss. This is where Betsy sewed the first American flag. At least, that's what they'd like you to believe. Some people are now saying that this is the wrong house, that Betsy's house was actually the one next door which was torn down. When told this, the contractor who tore it down said, "Oops!" So the house you see actually belonged to Betsy's next door neighbor, Myrtle Thunderbumper, who couldn't sew a stitch. Her sister-in-law, Hortense, could though and sewed many a lovely afghan for the boys going off to war.

Don't feel slighted at not seeing the right house, however, because surely Betsy and Myrtle must have gossiped over the back fence and shared many an intimate secret such as personal recipes, their thoughts on Martha Washington ("Did you see that tacky dress she wore to the inauguration?") and the real reason

Dolly Madison was considered the life of the party. Yes, the spirit of Betsy Ross lives in the Thunderbumper house even if Betsy didn't.

ENTERTAINMENT NOTE: Philadelphia is also the place where they filmed the movie *Rocky* and its 64 sequels starring Sylvester Pussycat. You remember the scene where he ran up the front steps of the Philadelphia Museum of Art? Well, they were going to use Independence Hall, but it has only two steps which somehow didn't seem quite as impressive. I personally feel they should have stopped after making *Rocky LXIII* because it was becoming increasingly difficult for Sly to get up those steps in his wheelchair. END OF ENTERTAINMENT NOTE.

Well, it's time now to conclude our visit to Philadelphia. I will miss it: the history, the art, the 12-second hand dryer and the Thunderbumper house. There's so much to do and see, that I barely scratched the surface and nearly got arrested for doing so. And best of all, seniors can ride the busses free, so I put on my long white beard, got on and rode for hours, not going anywhere, just unable to pass up such a bargain.

5 - HAVE YOU EVER BEEN TO ENGLAND?

England, the place where they're supposed to say, "What ho, Governor, pip, pip, cheerio and all that sort of rot!" Well, I've been to England several times and have never heard anybody say that. What they do say is, "Why can't you crazy Americans drive on the right side of the road?" "Listen," I say, "We do drive on the right; you drive on the left which is not right." They think that by driving on the left, they are right, but we know that right is right and left is wrong....Right? What? It's all very confusing. They're equally confused by their sports. What they call football is actually soccer, what they call rugby is actually football and what they call cricket is baseball. They're always mashing their niblets or giblets with their sticky wickets, or something like that. Pip, pip.

In England, you find a lot of history. The whole country just reeks with it, from the Tower of London to the Taj Mahal. The Tower of London is where they keep the Crown Jools . I went in there one day, and the crowd was moving so slowly that I thought I would liven the place up a bit by shouting, "Stick 'em up!" I now know why the British are not known for their sense of humor. They finally let me go, but only after my wife convinced them that I was a complete idiot.

Also, you know those Coldfeet Guards in their bright red tunics who stand around with bears on their heads? They're known for being so staunchly dedicated and not distracted by anything. Well, it's true. I gave one a *wet willy* one day, and he never flinched, just giggled slightly. Then, I tried doing my best animal imitations in front of him, but still he didn't budge. I thought I had him with my orangutan when I saw one eye flicker just a bit, but he never moved. One guard was so intent on standing at attention that one day a gang kidnapped the Queen, stole the Crown Jools and knocked down London Bridge, but he never moved a muscle. They later discovered that he was dead, but it's hard to tell the difference.

It was also in the Tower of London that many people were beheaded. That's the way they dealt with troublemakers long ago. If the king didn't like you, he'd say, "Off with his head!" King Henry VIII did that a lot, especially to his wives, of which he had about 143. I don't know why any girl would want to marry him though, knowing his reputation for separating his wives' heads from their bodies. As soon as he proposed, the girl should have hiked her skirts and run as fast and far as she could in the opposite direction. Of course, in those cumbersome dresses they wore back then, that might have been only about half a block.

The reason King Henry VIII didn't like his wives was because they wouldn't give him a son. He wanted a son he could play with and take fishing and to whom he could explain the facts of life and teach to flick boogers. But he had a lovely daughter by Anne Boleyn who was just like a boy. She could arm wrestle, whistle and beat up every member of the King's Guard. She grew up to become one of the greatest monarchs in British history: Kaiser Wilhelm. No. I'm just kidding. You know it was actually Queen Elizabeth I, the Virgin Queen. She was known as the Virgin Queen because whenever anything surprising happened, she would say, "Well, I never!"

It was during Queen Elizabeth I's reign that the English defeated the Spanish Armada, a fleet of 8 million ships that the Spanish sent to beat up the English. The Spanish were mad because Sir Walter Raleigh kept throwing his cigarette butts into the English Channel where they floated down to Spanish beaches and made a mess. The English prevailed by dropping Winston Churchill into the Channel creating a tidal wave and destroying the ships.

England is also the home of William Shakespeare. He wrote a lot of sonnets which are fourteen-line poems that make you want to faint. Most of them are about love such as, *It's Better to Have Loved and Lost...Much Better.* He also wrote 37 plays, though the authorship of them is sometimes in doubt. Some say he couldn't have written such sophisticated dramas because he was too short. I know this is true because I've been to his house, and the ceiling is so low that he must have been a Munchkin. I guess that's why the path to his house is a yellow brick road. Hmmm.

Shakespeare is buried in the Stratford River at Avon. No, that's not right. He's buried in Holy Trinity Church at Stratford on the Avon River. There's an inscription on his grave which reads: *Don't dare move my bones or I will rise up and haunt you for the rest of my life. I will grind you into powder and vultures will feast on your flesh until there's nothing left of you but a grease spot. You will be damned into Hell where you will be roasted on an open fire with chestnuts for all eternity.* Shakespeare invented hyperbole. I went out and had a stiff drink after that, and I certainly wasn't going to try moving his bones.

One cannot mention England without thinking of Sherlock Holmes, one of England's most famous historical figures. He lived at 221B Baker Street and was visited often by his loyal friend Dr. John Watson. Watson, the empty crucible yearning to be filled with the knowledge of his mentor, Holmes, who was always saying things like, "Elementary, my dear Watson," or, "The game is afoot!" He said these things to confuse Watson, and then he would snicker at the bewildered expression on Watson's face.

Not many people know this, but Watson was actually the brains of the outfit. That's right. Holmes never went beyond reform school, but Watson had a medical degree from the Attaboy School for Doctors, Plumbers and Lumberjacks. It was actually he who solved all the mysteries they encountered, but he let Holmes take all the credit because Holmes was bigger than he was and would have mashed his niblet if he objected.

Another historical wonder in England is Stonehenge, a pile of rocks standing in a circle. To this day, the English don't know what they were for, but they have some theories. One is that they were used by the Druids to play hide and go seek. Another is that they were placed there by aliens whom we know built the pyramids and then lost the City of Atlantis. My thought is that they just happened for no particular reason. That's right, like the theory of evolution. One day there were no stones there, just tiny little pebbles. Then, all of a sudden, they began to grow and evolved into the behemoths they are today after 800 million billion years. This is a much more plausible explanation than saying that aliens did it. Why would Mexicans go all the way to England just to build a circle of rocks? Ridiculous.

England was discovered by King Arthur and his knights of the round table. The table was round because they used to have fun spinning it and making bets to see which knight it would point to. Thus was born the game of spin the bottle. The knights were named Sir Lancelot, Sir Galahad, Sir Guinevere and a bunch of others. They used to go on crusades and quests. One of their famous quests was the one for the Holy Grail, but they never found it because they didn't know what a grail looked like.

To help find it, they hired the infamous adventurer, grave robber and obtainer of ancient antiquities, Rhode Island Schwartz, who was known for finding many famous treasures and icons. Among his more notable discoveries are Humpty Dumpty's wall, Whistler's mother's rocking chair, the last puzzle piece that's always missing, the Golden Gate Bridge and that tree that's always falling in the forest when no one's there to hear it.

Rhode Island Schwartz was rather eccentric. He always carried his I-Pod, and when he was on a heroic, adventurous mission, he would play this heroic, adventurous music to announce his presence. Sometimes his enemies would try to subvert his success, but they'd better watch out because he also carried his jump rope with him. He could flick the eye off a gnat with that thing. He was not invincible, however, for he had an irrational fear of butterflies. If one flew in his face, he would freak out and faint. He eventually did find the Grail in King Solomon's temple where it was being used as a door stop. Rhody liked it so much that he put it on his dresser and keeps his spare change in it.

King Arthur's kingdom was called Camelot. (No it's not a lot where you park your camel.) It was a magical kingdom later inherited by the Kennedy family. Numerous attempts have been made to discover its actual location, but King Arthur's personal magician, Mervin, cast a spell on it so nobody could find it. I think it's at Disney World mixed in with all those other kingdoms, like the Magic Kingdom, Fantasy Kingdom, Tomorrow Kingdom, Never-Never Kingdom, Busch Kingdom and Six Flags Kingdom.

In Wales, which is part of Great Britain, though no one has told the Welsh, there is a town named:

Llanfairpwllgwyngyllgogerychwyrndrobwllllantysiliogogogoch.

No, it's true, but do not try pronouncing it at home. You might hurt yourself. In Welsh, it means, *The town with the little white-washed church down the road by the river in which Shakespeare is buried while shepherds watched their flocks by night so olly-olly-in-free and a partridge in a pear tree, because Hootenanny Annie had a one-legged granny, y'all come, boop-boop-be-doop!*. Now say, *a skunk sat on a stump and thunk the stump stunk, but the stump thunk the skunk stunk.*

6- HOW TO DISCOVER AMERICA

First of all, you have to be Italian. This eliminates most people in the world. The Mafia eliminates the rest. Buford Lumpke from Arkansas tried to pass himself off as Italian so he could take credit for discovering America and went around saying things like *Pastafazool, Atsa soma spicy meataboll* and *Pizza*. Not many people believed him, though. We all know that America was discovered on the edge of the Earth by Cristoforo Columbo who played a detective on television, under the name *Peter Falk*. He later adopted the name *Christopher Columbus* to protect himself from all those criminals he had put in jail on flimsy evidence.

You also need a whole lotta money. Christopher Columbus didn't have any, so he first asked his neighborhood Godfather for some. The Godfather said, "How would you like to sleep with the fishes?" Columbus considered this an offer he could refuse. The next logical step was to ask the King and Queen of Spain, but they told him to get lost. He said, "That's what I'm trying to do. I want to lose myself in China which is just across the Atlantic Ocean."

Many people were afraid to sail across the ocean because they believed the earth was flat and they might sail right off the edge. Even some of Columbus' friends had sailed away and never returned, written or even called, but he said, "That's silly! I don't believe in that superstitious falderall!" (An old Italian expression.) He believed they were eaten by the Loch Ness Monster, Sasquatch or the Obamanibobble Snowman.

Finally, he convinced Queen Isabella of Spain to give him the money by promising to tie a rope around King Ferdinand's leg, so that if he did sail off the edge of the earth, Ferdy could pull him back up. A lot of people thought Columbus was crazy to go on this quest except his father who said, "I'm behind you, son, but would you mind paying me that 10 lire you owe me before you sail?"

The next thing you need in order to discover America is some ships. The recommended complement is three. It's little known that Columbus actually started with four, but that one did sail off the edge of the earth during its shakedown cruise. Columbus never reported this in his log; he put it down as *Sasquatch*. Columbus named his remaining ships the *Nina,* the *Pinta* and the *Andrea Doria*. He was going to name the first two *Titanic* and *Lusitania*, but those names were already taken.

In 1492, Columbus sailed the ocean blue. He actually sailed in 1493, but that doesn't rhyme with *blue* so he changed the date to make it easier for poets.

Besides, blue was his favorite color. The voyage to America was uneventful except for storms, whirlpools, sea serpents and being shelled by the German pocket battleship Graf Spee. Coulda been worse--coulda been the Bismarck.

Finally, they arrived at their destination, but it wasn't China, it wasn't even America. It was some place called *Hispaniola*. No one had ever heard of this place, so they told Columbus, "You have to go back and start over." He said, "No, let's just call it *India*. Nobody will know the difference, and everyone will think we made it around the world. We'll call the inhabitants *Indians* which is easier to say than *Hispanioliorians,* and it will be easier for John Wayne when he stars in all those Western movies he's gonna make." The Hispanioliorians said, "We're not Indians, we're Native Americans," but they were speaking Hispaniolish and Columbus couldn't understand them.

The next thing to do after discovering America is to give it a name. Columbus proclaimed, "I name this new land *Columbus*!" but people said, "You can't do that; the name's already being used by a city in Ohio." Then he said, "How 'bout Timbuktu?" but they shook their heads *No,* so he said, "West Timbuktu?"

While they were trying to decide what to call it, a man named Amerigoround Vespucci decided to draw a map of the new land. (His name is pronounced *A-merry-*

go-round *Vest-poochie*. Translation: *Dogs wearing vests are not allowed on the carousel*.) Even though he was a cartographer, a builder of carts, he liked to draw maps in his spare time. So he got out his Crayolas and started drawing, but he too could not think of a name for the new land.

While drawing, he was listening to some of his favorite 12 rpm records (the 78 had not been invented yet), and he heard a catchy tune called *God Bless America* written by Irving Stuttgart. Vespucci shouted, "That's it! I'll call it *Stuttgart!*" but some people who were still smarting over the Graf Spee incident said, "That sounds too German." His talking monkey, Abercrombie, suggested, "Why don't you name it after yourself, Amerigo?" (His friends and talking monkeys called him *Amerigo*.) He said, "Oh, okay, but I don't think many people will come to an unknown land called *Vespucci*." Meanwhile, Columbus was saying, "Xanadu? Liechtenstein? Graceland?" They took him away.

So, in summary, what you need in order to discover America is to be Italian, know the Queen of Spain, get some ships and an extremely long piece of rope and make people believe you're in India.

7 – SO, YOU WANT TO BE A TEACHER

*All hope abandon, ye who enter here!** You must also enjoy root canal surgery and having toothpicks driven under your fingernails. I was a teacher for what seemed like 450 years until they found out what was wrong with the school.

A typical school day starts with a period they call *Homeroom,* or more appropriately, *Let Me Copy Your Homework.* It is here that students struggle to wake up, get over their hangovers and plot those devious little schemes they hope to pull off during the day to drive their teachers crazy. Then students go to their various classes.

The rest of the day is spent in classes such as history, English and math where they put those schemes into practice.   One day a student asked his English teacher why he had to study English because he already knew how to talk good. The teacher replied that it was just to make them both miserable and that she hoped to continue his suffering right through summer school.

Someone once said, rather cleverly he probably believed, "Those who can, do--those who can't, teach." I would guess that the person who said that never had to prepare and execute a lesson plan or tried to manage a class full of teenagers whose raging testosterone (or the female equivalent) is ricocheting off the walls and whose only purpose in life seems to be frustrating the teacher's efforts to instill some inkling of knowledge into their rubbery heads.

Teaching wouldn't be so bad if it weren't for having to deal with all those students. During my teaching career, I came to believe that each student should sit in an ejector seat under the control of the teacher. Then when one of them becomes disruptive or disrespectful, push the old button and Ptooee! Gone! Of course, you then have to explain to the kid's parents why you launched their little darling into outer space. It's curious that some parents will ground their delinquent for eight years for painting the baby, wrecking the family car or throwing the wildest party since Roman Times, while they were out of town. Yet, those same parents won't admit that the little creep can do anything wrong in school.

In the latter 20th century, educational experts came up with a magic remedy to cure all learning disorders and solve all student-teacher problems which inhibit learning. It is called *Placebolin, the Wonder Drug.* It was believed that by pumping the student full of enough drugs to sedate the City of Chicago, somehow he would be a better student. No doubt, there are legitimate cases in which this works where the child has a learning disability such as ADD (or maybe too much ACDC or HDTV), but in other cases, students saw this as a foolproof excuse for releasing their pent-up hostility without fear of punishment. Instead of discipline, administrators would say, "Oh, it's okay because he's on Placebolin," or "Oh, he didn't take his Placebolin today," or "Oh, he just needs more Placebolin." What many of them needed was a trip behind the woodshed with dad.

A more effective use of Placebolin in schools would be to feed it to the teachers. In fact, this might even fulfill everyone's desires: fill the teachers with Placebolin, then let the inmates run the asylum. The students would be delirious over such freedom, administrators could smile smugly in the knowledge that they were allowing students to express themselves, and teachers wouldn't care because they'd be stoned and absolved of the responsibility to do any actual teaching.

I have met some hardworking, conscientious and responsible students in my time who help make the teaching profession bearable. Unfortunately, they suffer too when in a class with a slug whose main purpose is to see that no one learns anything that day. It takes only one--thus the need for the ejector seat. As a result, the teaching profession runs in weekly cycles of extreme emotional highs and lows. The highs come on weekends.

Sometimes there are amusing moments, like the time I asked a student how the shepherd was recognized in the Canterbury Tales. He replied, "Because he smelled like one." A boy wrote on a test one time, "The knight got down from his horse." I mischievously couldn't resist writing back, "You don't get down from a horse, you get down from a duck." I hope he's not in counseling today because of that. There was another student who outsmarted me one day when I asked him to define the word *procrastinate*. His answer: "I'll tell you tomorrow." I gave him an *A*. An excuse I received one day from a student who didn't have his homework was, "My dog peed on it," a clever twist on the classic, "My dog ate it."

So don't let me stop you from becoming a teacher, just think about what you're doing. PLEASE! And I'm not the only one saying this. A shared attitude toward school can be illustrated by the story of Harvey who woke up one day and said to his mother, "I don't want to go to school today! I don't like it! The teachers hate me, and all the students pick on me!" His mother said, "You have to go to school--you're the principal."

*Dante's *Inferno*

8 – WATCH OUT!
HERE COMES CHRISTMAS!

There was a time when it seemed that Christmas would never come. The days would drag on and on and on and o-o-o-o-o-n-n-n-n-n. Now, Christmas seems like a monthly holiday. What? Christmas again?! We just had it last month! Stores begin decorating right after Valentine's Day and competing for business by opening in the middle of the night. "We're opening at 4:00 a.m.!" "Well, we're opening at 3:00 a.m.!" "Pooh, we're opening at 2:59 a.m.!" Why don't they just stay open all night and make it easier on everybody? Then we wouldn't have to set our alarms to wake us just after we go to bed.

The stores call the day after Thanksgiving *Black Friday* because they hope to recoup all their losses for the year on that one day instead of declaring bankruptcy. It should be called *Black and Blue Friday* because that's what you look like after fighting with all the other shopping maniacs over a box of Tinkertoy which you could buy after Christmas for half price. Stores offer all kinds of sales and bombard you with coupons in the mail. One store offered a 99% discount for 99 seconds. You had to be really quick!

And radio stations don't help the situation by playing Christmas music all day long. They're the same songs we've heard 8 million times in our lives, and we still love them, but after a while they seem to merge into this endless musical montage of, *it's beginning to look a lot like home for the holidays because Frosty the red-nosed snowman is coming to town on a reindeer with silver bells to deck the halls with gold, frankincense and mistletoe, and a partridge in a pear tree, while angels on high sing rum-pum-pum on a midnight clear in a winter wonderland with Santa Claus roasting chestnuts in a one-horse open sleigh.* Hey!

The delicious foods of Christmas are especially noteworthy because we gain weight just smelling them. All kinds of pies, cakes, candies, cookies, turkey, ham, roast beast (Burp! 'Scuse me), shrimp, oysters, snails (Ugh!), pheasant under plexi-glass, elephant ears, chocolate-covered grasshoppers, monkey brains and tofu. Yum! Yum!

While gorging yourself on one or more of these tasty treats, you may want to sit down and watch one of your favorite Christmas movies. This is where you and people everywhere learn the stories of Christmas. We know of Eversneezer Scrooge, the grouchy old miser who wouldn't buy his nephew, Tiny Tim, a B-B gun for Christmas until Clarence, the Ghost of Christmas Out-of-a-Job, told him he was going to croak. Then he left all of his money to the bishop and his wife who wanted a cathedral for Christmas. An angel named Dudley Dashing came down and challenged them to a snowball fight. Afterwards, they all had lunch at Michelle's and went ice skating.

Agnes Pennypincher, the crochety old millionairess, was going to build the cathedral until she heard that George Bailey had lost 8 thousand dollars on a snow-removal scheme and decided to help him out. He had previously sought help from Harry Potter, another grumpy old skinflint, who told him to go jump in the river. George said, "No, I'm enjoying life," to which Potter replied, "That's wonderful!"

Clark Greaseball, who lived at the airport, wanted a swimming pool for Christmas so he dug a hole, but his brother-in-law who had the I.Q. of a semi-colon, emptied his toilet into the hole, causing Clark to utter a bad word. He had learned it from his neighbor, Ralphie, who was a potty-mouth. Ralphie's mother made him stick his tongue onto a frozen flagpole as punishment after triple-dog-daring him. Ralphie's little brother, Randy, ate like a pig, so when his father won a lamp shaped like a leg of lamb, Randy ate it.

A little girl who lived on 34th Street asked her friend, Kris Kringle, for a house for Christmas, but it wouldn't fit into her stocking. Kris was on trial for believing he was the Easter Bunny, and they were about to send him away until the Post Office stepped in and sent him all these letters proving that he was actually Santa Claus. He had wondered why there were elves in his house making all these toys which were piling up. Kris was very glad to receive the letters until he noticed that they were all stamped *Postage Due.* He immediately jumped on the Polar Express, had hot chocolate and went back home.

The main thing we learn from watching all those movies is that every time we hear a bell ring, it's either the front doorbell or the telephone, and we're usually in the bathtub.

Finally, on Christmas Eve, we're sitting down with our loved ones in front of the blazing tree (I told you it was too close to the fireplace!), with the Christmas montage playing softly in the background, *Fa-ra-ra-ra-ra-ra-ra-ra-ra,* and snow piling up hiney deep to a nine-foot Indian. Wonderfully, in spite of all the distracting commercial sights, sounds, smells and tastes of Christmas, we still feel deep in our hearts the real meaning of Christmas: that it is, after all, a truly Holy Night.

9 – ANTONY, CLEOPATRA AND A GUY NAMED JULIUS

Before getting into the complex relationships among these three characters, some history of Rome is in order. The Roman Empire began as a city founded by Romulus and Uncle Remus in 753 B.C. They argued over who would be the first king, and Romulus won because Uncle Remus was too busy telling stories about Br'er Rabbit, Br'er Fox and Br'er Elephant. Otherwise, the city would have been named Reme, not Rome.

By the first century B.C., the City of Rome had grown into a great nation, so Julius Caesar and his cronies, Pompadour and Autocrassius, formed the *First Triumvirate*, but soon they were fighting with each other over how to make a salad. Caesar emerged triumphant which was lucky for us--can you imagine going to a restaurant and ordering a Pompadour salad?! As a result, Caesar was made dictator for life! Wow! What more pompous a title could you want, except maybe *Exalted Great High Potentate of the Mystic Order of the Universe.*

While browsing through some travel brochures one day, Caesar spied a picture of Cleopatra, Queen of the Nile. That's in Egypt. He had never before beheld such a beautiful countenance, except once in a pet basset hound he had as a child, so he freaked out and exclaimed, "That's the girl for me!" He had always wanted to see the Nile, the Pyramids and the Grand Canyon, so he immediately packed his bags and headed for Egypt. His wife, Catastrophe, didn't seem to mind at all. Romans of the time were very liberal in matters of this sort, and besides, it got him out of the house.

Ah, Egypt! The mysterious land of the pharaohs, the Nile, the Pyramids and sand in your shorts. A mere mention of the Valley of the Kings conjures up images of vast riches and mummies. Every once in a while, one of the mummies would come to life, stalk around and scare the papyrus out of everybody. The most famous mummy is King Tut whose tomb was discovered, virtually intact, by Howard Carter in 1922. The curse inscribed on Tut's tomb is so horrible to contemplate that I dare not repeat it here! Suffice it to say, if I did, you'd have to change your pants. It is in Egypt where they worship various gods like Osiris bin Laden and Anubis. Anubis looks like a dog because a dyslexic priest once told the Egyptians, "You should all believe in Dog!"

Upon arriving in Egypt, Caesar discovered that Cleopatra was in a power struggle with her brother, Deuphius (pronounced Doo-fuss), who was trying to assassinate her. (He also discovered that the photo of Cleopatra he had seen was rather dated, and she now looked more like Dumbledore!) For safe keeping, Caesar had Cleopatra rolled up in a rug where she nearly suffocated. She emerged gasping and choking and shouted, "What the heck's the matter with you--are you crazy?!" Caesar had never been spoken to like that before, but he liked it and immediately fell in love with her. Soon they had a baby whom they called Caesarian because he was born through the new birth process which had become popular: Pilates.

Caesar was eventually called away from Egypt to deal with a crisis in Gaul where he crossed the Rubik's Cube. After he conquered Gaul, the Senate became fed up with his *ambition,* thus the expression: *He had a lot of Gaul!* Caesar had been doing stand-up comedy at the forum for some time now and wanted to move on to radio, TV and movies. (Movies of the time consisted of flip cards.) So the Senate got together and bumped him off on the *Ides of March* in 44 B.C. *(Ides of March is a secret code meaning, If you're smart, you'll stay home today.* Evidently, Caesar did not know the code.) While Brutus, one of his assassins, was stabbing him, Caesar said, "Et tu Brute'?" which means "Let's do lunch," but he said it in Latin: "Jeet jet? No, ju? No, squeet!"

At Caesar's funeral, his friend Marc Antony delivered his famous funeral oration in which he said, "Julius Caesar was a wise old geezer; he washed his face in the ice cream freezer." Oops! Wrong quote. He actually said, "Friends, Romans, countrymen, lend me your ears!" He said this because he was trying to drum up business for his medical practice. He was an ENT specialist in partnership with Cyrano de Bergerac and Count Dracula. Cyrano handled noses (Ich!), and Dracula looked after people's throats (Tee hee!). This left ears for Marc Antony which is good because it would have sounded rather silly for him to say, "Friends, Romans, countrymen, lend me your noses!"

After Caesar was kilt, Antony formed an alliance with two other guys, Gaius Gingivitis and Cassius Clay, called the *Second Triumvirate*. Since it followed the First Triumvirate, this was an especially clever name. But wouldn't you know it? Soon they were fighting with each other over who was going to get Cleopatra. What was it with those Romans? They couldn't get along with anybody.

Antony went to Egypt to claim Cleopatra but was pursued by Caesar's successor, *Octopus*. The forces of Antony and Cleopatra were defeated by Octopusses (Octopus's? Octopot's?) army at the Battle of Midway in 31 B.C., so Tony and Cleo ran away. Realizing the end was near, they both committed suicide, Antony by running himself through with a burning shish kebab spear and Cleopatra by asp. (I will forego the obvious pun here.)

10 – THE STORY OF FLIGHT – PART 1

Of all the wonders of nature which man has beheld since the beginning of time, there is one that has captivated and bewildered him more than any other: Women! No, that's not right. Well, actually it is right, but in addition, there is something else: Birds in flight. Sounds kinda boring by comparison, doesn't it? But I'm stickin' with it.

The wonder of flight has always filled man with a burning desire to emulate birds by learning to fly and lay eggs. Since Icarus flew too near the sun, man has been trying over and over again to fly, but with a better sense of direction, and many men have laid eggs in the process. Some have attached giant wings to their arms and jumped off of cliffs without real success. They were fine until they hit bottom. Others have built machines which huffed and puffed and then fell all apart without going anywhere.

Then along came Orville and Wilbur Wright who ran a bicycle shop in Dayton, OH, where they developed one of the most marvelous inventions in the history of mankind: the flying bicycle. To advertise their success, they used the slogan, "Forget the plane, take a bike!" The flying bicycle wasn't very popular, though, because it was nothing more than a bicycle with wings attached and wouldn't really fly no matter how fast you pedaled.

Rather than being discouraged, however, Orville and Wilbur continued their efforts and experimented in various ways to achieve flight. Wilbur used to glue bird feathers all over his body and then jump off the barn. He couldn't fly, but boy could he build a nest. He kept assuring people that someday he would fly, but they just yelled, "Horse feathers!" He thought they were encouraging him, so he covered himself with horse feathers which didn't enable him to fly, but did give him a strong desire to run in the Kentucky Derby. It also increased his appetite for oats. People began calling him *Wacky Wilbur*.

Then on December 17, 1903, he accomplished something that no one has ever done before or since. He finished reading *War and Peace*. Then right after that, he went out and flew the first manned aircraft in history at Kitty Hawk, NC. To capitalize on his fame, he sold rides to people and established a tradition that airlines still practice to this day: he lost their luggage. They no longer called him *Wacky Wilbur* but other names, instead.

There have been many memorable milestones in aviation history, none more significant than the first flight across the Atlantic Ocean which occurred on May 20-21, 1927. A mention of the initials *C. L.* brings to mind the name Salma Hayek. I know those are not her initials, but she comes to mind anyway. The real person I'm thinking of here is Charles Lindbergh, *The Lone Eagle*. All alone, he flew his plane *The Spirit of Christmas* from Roosevelt Field on Long Island to Le Bourget Field in Paris, France, a distance of nearly 3,600 miles. All he had with him was a sandwich and a cup of water--no radio, no CD player, no GPS and best of all, no backseat driver.

People asked Lindbergh why he wanted to go to France which was full of French people. He told them because it was also full of snails, in addition to people, which he loved saute'ed in butter--snails, not people. Upon arriving in Paris, Lindbergh was besieged by throngs of people swarming around his plane and shouting at the tops of their lungs. He couldn't make out what they were saying until he turned off the engine and heard, "Elvis! Elvis!"

After his triumphant return to America, Lindbergh was given a ticker-tape parade up Fifth Avenue. That's where you ride in an open car and people dump their trash on top of you. Oh, it's a great honor reserved only for the elite! They gave Lindbergh the nickname *Lucky Lindy,* and we even have a dance named after him: The Bunny Hop.

Almost as famous is Amelia Earhart, the well-known aviatrix. That means *female pilot.* No one knows why she's famous except that she disappeared. J'ever notice that some people in life become famous for simply disappearing? In addition to Amelia, there is Judge Roy Bean, Jimmy Hoffa, Calvin Coolidge, Joe Biden and Dr. Livingstone, I presume. Actually, Amelia Earhart is justly famous because she became the first woman to fly across the Atlantic Ocean. At first, she was reluctant to do so since it already had been done by Lindbergh, but then she heard that there was a sale on French fashions and was off like a shot!

On June 1, 1937, Amelia Earhart set out on an around-the-world flight from Miami, FL, but disappeared over the Pacific Ocean and is still missing. It is my belief that, because of increased air traffic today, she may still be stacked up over L.A.X. awaiting landing instructions.

An amusing story in aviation history is that of Douglas *Wrong Way* Corrigan, a pilot who intended to fly from Brooklyn, NY, to Long Beach, CA, but ended up in Dublin, Ireland. That is funnier than I could ever make it, so I will not try.

11 – THE STORY OF FLIGHT – PART 2

After all the early, ground-breaking advancements from the Wright Brother's success at Kitty Hawk to *Wrong Way* Corrigan's flight to Dublin, the story of flight really took off. (Is that a pun?) As quickly as you could say, "Fasten your seatbelts," "Non fumare," or "Where's my barf bag?" we moved right into the jet age. The main thing I remember about the jet age is the joke Red Skelton used to tell about the two seagulls, Gertrude and Heathcliffe, who were flying along one day when one of the new jet planes whooshed by. Heathcliffe remarked, "Wow! That bird was really moving!" Gertrude explained, "You'd move that fast too if your tail was on fire!" Laugh? I thought I'd drop the baby!

The hilarious jet age was followed promptly by the space age. Outer space: that's where they keep all those planets, big round rocks floating about trying to stay out of each other's way. Let's see, there's Mercury, Venus, Earth, Mars, Jupiter, Saturn, Bolivia, Pluto and Goofy. Technically speaking, Pluto is no longer a planet. It used to be but its lease expired, so it had to stop calling itself a planet. In fact, it may have to leave the solar system because respectable planets will have nothing to do with it.

At one point, someone suggested that we send space craft to these rocks and see what's there. They said, "We can send monkeys." Others said, "Why risk monkeys, we can send men." They then agreed to send little probes and rovers with cameras attached to show what they discovered. We already knew that there were Martians on at least one planet, but when we tried to take their picture, the Martians hid so we couldn't see them. All we saw was rocks.

After hearing that we were in the space age, the people at NASA (National Airplanes and Spaceships Anonymous) decided that we should go to the moon, so they put an ad in the paper: *Wanted. People willing to be locked into a tiny capsule and placed on the tip of a gigantic rocket filled with 800 million tons of highly explosive liquid oxygen while we set fire to it.* Not surprisingly, there were few applicants, but very surprisingly, they did receive 7. I wonder if they read the fine print.

Before shooting for the moon, however, a suborbital flight was necessary. This is where you shoot a rocket up high but let it fall back to earth without actually achieving any kind of orbit. It is the equivalent of bouncing really high on a pogo stick or a trampoline. Trampolines are fun! You can bounce up and down, do somersaults and try all kinds of tricks. What's really entertaining is watching those funny videos on TV where they show someone bouncing on a trampoline who suddenly loses control and crashes right through his neighbor's bedroom window or flies off into the swimming pool. Sometimes, he will get his leg caught, almost ripping it off, or land on his head, nearly breaking his neck. Either way, it's really funny!

While America was preoccupied with suborbital flying, the Soviet Union, as Brazil was then called, was making great strides in advancing the progress of man. They put Sputnik (a pea-sized satellite) into orbit, sent a man around the earth, performed a spacewalk, and invaded Hungary, Czechoslovakia, Uruguay and probably some other countries I've overlooked. Remarkably, they accomplished all this while keeping the Soviet people completely uninformed. Meanwhile, the American people weren't used to placing second to the Soviets and wondered why we couldn't have done those things. All we accomplished was a suborbital flight and invading Arkansas and Alabama.

Then the day came when we would eclipse all other air and space achievements. We opened Disney World in Florida. Space Mountain? Don't get me started! My head is still spinning! Then we actually topped this feat by really going to the moon in July of 1969. Three astronauts, we'll just call them Nate, Bozz and Michelle, were rocketed into lunar orbit, and while Michelle stayed with the *mother ship* orbiting the moon, Nate and Bozz descended to the lunar surface in the *Eagle* module. Who can forget Nate's immortal words as they touched down, "Look out! We're gonna crash! Eeeyyyaaahhhaaiiee!!" When he regained his composure, he calmly announced, "Tranquility Base here. The Eagle needs changing!" It was enough to bring tears to a steer's ears.

Then came the monumental question of who would actually be the first person to step onto the surface of the moon. Nate and Bozz had already determined through the scientific process of *Rock, Paper, Scissors* that Nate would be first, but the onboard computer malfunctioned and wouldn't open the door. The computer had been nicknamed MALCOM, short for *malfunctioning computer.*

MALCOM'S refusal to open the door led to this exchange:

Nate: "Okay, MAL, open the module door."

MAL: "No way, Dave. I'll open it when I'm good and ready."

Nate: "The name's *Nate,* and why are you disobeying me?"

MAL: "You're always bossing me around, and I'm sick and tired of it. I'm only human, you know."

Nate: "No you're not, you're a machine--and if you don't open this door, I'm gonna sing *A Bicycle Built For Two* !"[1]

With that, MAL screamed, "No, no, not that!" held his ears and immediately opened the door causing Nate to fall out the door and down the ladder, landing on his face. Looking up from his prone position, Nate moaned, "That's one small step for a man, one painful plunge for mankind...and I want my Mommy!" His quote was slightly altered for public consumption, and the imprint of his painfully distorted face remains in the lunar dust for all eternity.

After 50 years of space exploration, including nine trips to the moon and numerous missions to Earth and the other planets in a fruitless search for intelligent life, NASA has garnered a lovely collection of moon rocks. Considering the overall cost of the entire space program, each rock must be worth about 50 billion dollars. One rock in particular is the object of intense curiosity and may call into question all the time, effort and expense, for an inscription thereon reads, "Made in China."   When told this, the Chinese Premier just smiled.

12 – WHERE IS THE CONTINENT OF AR(C)TICA?

The planet Earth is constructed of a whole bunch of condiments...I mean condominiums...no I mean continents...and oceans. At last count, there were 13 or 14 continents and some 9 or 10 oceans. At least, that's what it looks like when you view a map or globe. However, according to my trusty World Encyclopedia of Borneo, there are only seven (7) continents and five (5) oceans. You don't really believe that do you?

Let's discuss the continents first. The supposed seven, alphabetically in order of height, are: Africa, Antarctica, Asia, Australia, Europe, North America and South America. Seems like they ran out of names beginning with *A* after the first four, then they panicked and chose the name *Europe* without giving it any logical thought. Sounds like a burp. The names *North* and *South America* I can understand, thanks to Amerigoround Vespucci (or was it Captain America?).

Africa is where they keep all the African elephants and the country of South Africa is there, so that's probably where they got the name. Asia is the largest continent, which is good because that's where you find a lot of very large countries like China, India and most of Russia. If it were any smaller, they wouldn't fit. The rest of Russia is in Europe which is inhabited by some minor countries like Switzerland, Liechtenstein and Texas. So it seems like Europe should be called *Asia Minor*, but I understand that Asia Minor is located somewhere completely different, so let's not even go there. (Wouldn't that make an eighth continent?) Just where do Europe and Asia divide anyway, and where the heck or what the heck is Transvaal?

Australia is the coolest of the continents because, first of all, it's occupied by only one country which, coincidentally, is also named *Australia*, so it doesn't have any neighbors to fight with as there are on other continents.   Here you find some of the coolest animals: kangaroos, wombats, coca cola bears, platypusses (platypi?) and eucalyptusseses. God was in a frisky mood when he created Australia. Best of all, Crocodile Dundee lives there, and you know he's cool. ("That's not a knife--this is a knife.")[2] I figure a continent that cool can pick any name it wants.

Australia also has these sticks which are impossible to throw away. When you try, they come right back to you. This makes the game of *fetch* very boring. You don't need your dog, so there aren't many dogs in Australia. They have *dingos* instead, whatever they are.

This leaves *Antarctica,* a large continent covered in ice which has caused it to slide to the bottom of the earth. There is nothing there but some penguins, little birds all dressed up in little tuxedos with no place to go. They aren't all little, though. Some penguins get rather large, and they're called *emperor penguins* because they think they run the place. Since there's nothing else there, they probably do. I've purposely left *Antarctica* for last because it has a lot to answer for.

I've also switched to a new paragraph here because this may take a while. First of all, I don't like the *c* in the middle of the names Arctic and Antarctic-- it's takes extra effort to pronounce them, so I'm just going to leave it out from now on. Secondly, the name *Antartic* (see, I told you) means *the opposite* of *Artic.* (You know, like *antifreeze* is the opposite of *freeze,* *antimatter* is the opposite of *unclematter* and *antidisestablishmentarianism* is the opposite of--that other word.) Therefore, it would follow that *Antartica* is the opposite of *Artica,* which means that there must be an *Artica,* right!? Well, where is it? It should be on top of the world where Santy Claus lives, but the only thing there is a frozen ice cap with nothing underneath.

This is a question that has puzzled me, and I know you, ever since I learned to pronounce the middle *c.* There's got to be an *Artica* somewhere! Is it hiding under Greenland which is a big island in the Artic region? I think they've looked there but haven't found it. After thorough consideration, I have concluded that *Artica* must have been the former name of the Lost Continent of Atlantis, and that's where it is...lost. I know you're glad to have that question answered for you. Also, doesn't it feel good not having to pronounce that *c* in the names of *you-know-what?*

By the way, since Greenland is so big, why is it called an island and not a continent? Maybe, since an ocean is a large body of salty *water*, a continent can be defined as a large body of salty *dirt*, and Greenland just isn't salty enough. And why is a country that's all frozen in the middle called *Greenland* in the first place? They wanted to name it *Iceland,* but since that name was already taken, they mistakenly asked a committee for advice. Other committee recommendations were *Bermuda, Neptune* and *Frieshapanzoffland..* I guess *Greenland's* not so bad after all. Had they named it *Artica,* I wouldn't have had to write this article.

In addition to continents and islands, there are other land masses which make up the earth; for example, isthmusses and peninsulasses. Another word I don't like because it's hard to pronounce is *isthmus.* Any civilized society would simply say *ismus,* so let's do so from now on. And I don't understand *atoll* at all. I think an atoll is tinier than an island with no room to stand on it, so people who live on one have to hang on for dear life. Pity the Azoreoreites.

Concerning changes in spelling, George Bernard Shaw, a severe critic of English language spelling, once said he could spell the word *fish* as *ghoti* and no one could prove him wrong. He took the *gh* from words like *enough (f)*, the *o* from *women (i)*, and *ti* from words like *nation (sh)*. Result: ghoti=fish. Perhaps I should mention that George was also a proponent of the flat earth theory, so maybe we shouldn't rely too heavily on his authority.

That just about clears up any questions concerning continents and other land masses. But while I'm here, let's talk about oceans which cover over 70% of the earth's surface and should make you wonder why the deserts are so dry. Seems like the water would have soaked through by now. As I mentioned earlier, the Borneo Encyclopedia identifies five oceans: Antartic, Artic (no *c's*, see?) Atlantic, Indian and Pacific. Lately, some people have been trying to change the name of the Antartic Ocean to the *Southern* Ocean. This is a stupid idea. I mean, they don't seem concerned that there is an Antartica but no Artica; however, we do have Artic and Antartic Oceans, so why screw up what little consistency we have by changing one of the names? Has anybody asked the penguins how they feel about it?

As with land masses, there are other bodies of water besides oceans. There are seas, lakes, rivers, streams, babbling brooks, puddles and cricks, not to mention tributaries. But don't get me started on seas versus oceans. Too late! God made oceans salty so people wouldn't drink them dry. (This is unfortunate for people who are stranded at sea and can't drink the water. Oh well, they should have planned ahead.) There are also many large seas of salt water which could be called oceans such as the Mediterranean and the Caribbean. Just where gulfs, bays and fjords fit into this picture, I'm not sure. (*fjords* looks like a typo, doesn't it?)

This reminds me of a teacher I once had who pronounced *Carib'bean* with the emphasis on the second syllable which I had never heard before. I always said, "Carribbe'an," emphasizing the third syllable. So in class one day when she asked, "What should one never call it?" I proudly answered, "Caribbe'an," but she said, "No, Gulf of Mexico."   I think she set me up.

The status of seas versus lakes is also curious. We have the Black Sea and the Caspian Sea which are land-locked but still called *seas.* Yet, the Great Lakes, also land-locked, are not called *seas.* If they're so *Great*, why not?

Ancient mariners and pirates used to brag about *sailing the seven seas.* Well, a quick calculation reveals that in addition to the five oceans, there are at least eleven seas: Adriatic, Aegean, Arabian, Black, Caribbean, Caspian, China, Holy, Japan, Mediterranean and Red. So if you try to pick just seven, it could be quite aggravating. Maybe that's why pirates have such nasty dispositions and go around saying, "Aargh!" all the time.

13 – LIFE AFTER A&E

When God created Adam and Eve in the Garden of Eden, He promised them a life of leisure and luxury. Everything was to be provided for them. They would never have to work, wear clothes, pay taxes, buy insurance, wash the car, go to the market, visit in-laws, attend PTA, mow the lawn, shovel snow, watch reality TV, see fat people in bikinis, change diapers, breathe someone else's smoke, receive unwanted phone calls, wait for a table, tip anybody, pay dues to any clubs or organizations, get stuck in traffic or listen to Rush Limbaugh, Jehovah's Witnesses, loud-mouthed politicians and screeching, unintelligible noise passed off as music. All they had to do was be fruitful and multiply. This very same life style was to be passed down to all of A&E's descendants--that is, until they broke God's commandment and ate the forbidden fruit. THANKS A LOT ADAM AND EVE!!

After A&E were expelled from the Garden of Eden, their descendants overspread the earth, migrating in all directions. God saw that many of them were turning to an evil life of sin. They were engaging in all forms of debauchery: throwing trash in the streets, spitting on sidewalks, posting bills, trespassing, sticking gum under their theater seats and not waiting for the vehicle to come to a complete stop before exiting. So

God repented of his creation and planned to destroy all life on earth.

However, there was one good man among them named Noah who had a wife and three sons, Larry, Moe and Curly. God warned Noah that it was going to rain like something crazy. You know, felines and canines. He told Noah to build an Ark.

Noah asked, "What's an Ark? Is it anything like an aardvark?"

God said, "What's an aardvark?"

Noah answered, "You know, the first animal in the dictionary."

God replied, "Oh yeah, that one. I forgot."

He then explained that the Ark was to be a big boat, bigger than the Queen Mary, which would house two of every animal on earth. Noah said, "Do I have to bring bats 'cause they're really ugly?"

God said, "Every animal."

"Well how 'bout bugs and spiders? My wife doesn't like spiders."

God re-emphasized, "Everything, except maybe platypuses because I think I really goofed there."

So Noah began building his boat. It was a bright, sunny day, so the people round about thought this was the funniest thing they had ever seen, except the time President Ford conked a guy on the head with a golf ball. Then it began to rain, and when the rain turned into a flood, the people started begging Noah to take them aboard. However, Noah just stuck his tongue out at them, put his thumbs in his ears and wiggled his fingers. It felt good. Soon the Ark was afloat on an ocean that overwhelmed the entire world. The only people left alive were Noah, his wife, his sons' wives and Larry, Moe and Curly, who passed the time poking each other in the eye, hitting each other on the head and punching Curly in the stomach to the sound of a bass drum.

After 40 days and several nights, the Ark came to rest on top of Mount Suribachi. Noah sent out a raven and a dove. The raven went to Baltimore, but the dove returned with an olive branch in its mouth. Noah said, "Ah, good, now we can make martinis, and I really need one." When Noah and his sons got off the boat, it was very muddy everywhere, but they had remembered to bring their galoshes, so it was okay, except Mrs. Noah yelled, "Don't you track that mud in here! Haven't I got enough to do, cleaning up after all these other animals?!"

God told Noah and his sons to be fruitful, multiply and replenish the earth which they set about doing with great gusto! From that day forward, they produced six billion descendants, and boy were they tired! That's about one a week, isn't it?

Before long, the earth was once again full of people. However, some of Noah's descendants had settled in the towns of Sodom and Glockamora two of the most evil places on earth. There, they lived wicked and violent lives. Not only were they committing their ancestors' sins, they were also wearing brown shoes with black socks and refusing to close their covers before striking. It was literally Hell on earth! Well, God simply would not stand for this, so He dropped an H-bomb on them and blew them all to smithereens--all except Lot, a good man, whom God had warned to get out of town with his wife. Lot told his wife not to look back, but sadly, she looked anyway and was turned into a pillow.

One race of people that Noah and his sons produced were the Israelites who were living a happy and productive life until they were cast into slavery by the nation of Egypt. The pharaoh of Egypt at the time was King Tut who was very cruel to the Israelites and forced them to make bricks out of mud so he could build the pyramids. He was originally going to build three-dimensional trapezoids, but was advised that pyramids would be quicker and would look better on postcards, so he said okay.

But just in time, God found another good man. Yay! That's three in about 4,000 years. His name was Moses. There is great irony in the story of Moses because he had been cast adrift by his mother in the bull hockies when the Israelites were being suppressed and was found, adopted and raised by King Tut himself. When Tut discovered that Moses was actually a Hebrew, he was very angry, stamped his feet and wouldn't come out of his room for a whole month. Didn't you see the movie? By the time the king emerged from his room, Moses had skedaddled.

Years later, Moses was hanging out with his sheep (he was very lonely) when a nearby bush burst into flame so suddenly that he jumped right out of his shoes and socks! Remembering his Boy Scout training, Moses threw dirt on the bush to put it out, but it wouldn't go out, so Moses knew he was in the presence of God. God commanded Moses to return to Egypt and set His people free. King Tut had died by this time, and his son, King Tut-Tut, was now on the throne of Egypt. When Moses arrived, Tut-Tut asked him what he wanted.

Moses replied, "Let my people go!"

The pharaoh scoffed, "Tut, tut, don't make me laugh."

Then he laughed. "Even if you called down hail, plagues of locusts, frogs and flies and turned the Nile River to blood, I would not let your people go."

Well, that's exactly what Moses did, so Tut-Tut said, "Okay, you can go."

Then Moses and all the Israelites left Egypt and headed for the Promised Land, the Land of Milk and Honey, Miami, Florida.

After they left, Pharaoh Tut-Tut had second thoughts and regretted his decision to let the people go.

His advisors said, "If you had had your second thoughts first, this wouldn't have happened."

Tut-Tut said, "If I had had my second thoughts first, then they wouldn't be second thoughts, would they?"

This debate continued for a few minutes, until the pharaoh ordered his advisors' entrails torn out. Then he mounted a large army and pursued the Israelites in an attempt to bring them back.

By this time, however, the Israelites had reached the Red Sea where they stopped and couldn't go any farther because the drawbridge was up. Just as pharaoh and his army were about to descend on them,

Moses looked up to heaven and shouted, "Now what?" With that, the waters of the Red Sea parted and the Israelites escaped, but unlike Noah, they didn't need their galoshes because even the bottom was dry. Then when King Tut-Tut's army attempted to cross the Red Sea, it closed up with a big *splash*, and they all perished. The Israelites cheered and applauded and thanked God for the entertainment.

Afterward, Moses went up on Mount Kilimanjaro to receive the Ten Commandments. God asked Moses, "What do you want?"

Moses replied, "I'm here to get the Ten Commandments,"

God said, "Well, they're not ready yet. Come back later."

When Moses returned, God gave him the Ten Commandments and told him, "As soon as you learn these, come back and I'll give you ten more."

But Moses knew he wouldn't be back because the people would never be able to follow all those commandments, especially the ones about not coveting things. And boy was he right!

Eventually, Moses' people reached their destination and established the great nation of Israel, but their troubles with Egypt and their other Arab neighbors were far from over. But that's a story for another time.

14 – CARS AND TRUCKS AND THINGS THAT GO *BUMP* IN THE NIGHT

Every little boy enjoys cars and trucks and things that go. I did, my son did, as did his son, and every boy before and since has been equally fascinated by them. They especially love to race them and crash them into each other. It is from this early experience that boys develop the techniques they will use when they begin driving real cars in later life.

The car was invented by Henry Ford, at least he developed the internal combustion engine, even though the Russians and certain other nations high on exhaust fumes try to claim that honor. Coincidentally, there is an automobile named after Henry Ford, and one of the most successful companies in history which has provided employment for many thousands of people still bears the name of that car: The Henry Motor Company.

Henry Ford used to play with cars and trucks when he was a boy, and he always wondered what made them go. Someone told him, "Because you push them," and he said, "Oh, yeah." Then someone gave him a windup car that moved without pushing it, and this gave him his monumental inspiration. He invented a life-sized, windup car. The key was rather large and hard to wind, unless you carried a professional wrestler with you, but once you wound it up, it would go for many feet before stopping.

People marveled at this new invention and everybody wanted one, so Ford had to begin mass production which involved something called *an assembly line*. This is a bunch of people in a row, each one performing a specific task as the car passes before them. One person would put on the wheels, the next the bumpers, then the ash trays, etc. One person in the line was responsible for cutting the holes in the floor of the Flintstone model. The last person in the line would spray the assembled car with new-car smell.

The most critical job was installing the key. It had to be meticulously inserted and calibrated for maximum wind. It was also a rather dangerous job, for occasionally the spring would pop while being wound, sending the winder flying off into another county. It was from this accident of industry that the concept of the modern catapult was developed, an innovation which changed the hobby of waging war forever.

Playing with trucks is even more fun than cars because you can crash them together even harder, especially in real life. It's fun watching the truck commercials on television: "Our truck can climb sheer, vertical rock cliffs by utilizing the optional anti-gravity frenistator!" "Oh yeah, well our trucks don't bother climbing the cliff, they go right through it!" Then they'll show you a truck driving over a field of four-foot boulders. The trucks are given clever, descriptive names like *The Road Ravager* or *The Boulder Basher.* The names usually alliterate, too, and make you want to go right out and buy one.

In addition to cars and trucks, another thing that goes is the train. Years ago, virtually every boyhood home would have a Christmas train garden. Don't call a permanent train *layout* a *garden*, though, because the hobbyist will yell at you and make you feel like the lowest form of plant life on earth. "IT'S NOT A GARDEN, IT'S A LAYOUT YOU BIG, FAT, STUPID IGNORAMUS YOU!!!" However, the Christmas variety can be called a garden because it is temporary just for the season.

What joy a Christmas garden brings to the boy and his family! I say *boy* because not many girls expressed an interest in model trains, although a leading model train manufacturer did market a train specifically for girls one time by coloring it *PINK!* That was the only time because nobody bought one. I think the idea for this came from the same guy who later changed the formula for a popular soft drink much to their horror and chagrin when it made people regurgitate. I wonder if he's the same one who designed the blue football field at an Idaho university which makes my eyes go all bleary when I try to watch a game. If so, he's now probably panhandling on skid row.

The airplane is another example of something that goes. You can read the fascinating history of the development of the airplane in the captivatingly-brilliant and thoroughly-researched article, *The Story of Flight, Part 1,* included in this volume.

I chose the title for this current piece because I thought it was kind of clever, not really thinking of how I was going to tie the two subjects together. Anyone who has ever spent the night in a New York hotel room has likely heard cars and trucks literally going *bump, crash or kablooey* in the middle of the night. The noise is often mingled with screams, gunshots and the sound of trash men throwing the cans and dumpsters off the roof to explode right below your window at 4:00 a.m. Otherwise, cars and trucks have little relationship to things that go bump in the night. Do ghosts drive cars and trucks? No, I don't think so unless you count the guy who falls asleep at the wheel and will soon become a ghost.

One common trait amongst cars and trucks and things that go bump in the night is that they all can scare the living crap out of you. If you've ever driven with someone who aims their car instead of driving it, and every time he or she approaches an oncoming vehicle your life flashes before you, then you have some idea of what I mean. It's as if they have a death wish, but you wish they would wish for death at a more opportune time, like when you're not in the car.

Things that go bump in the night are regarded by many people, not as fearful, but as thrilling, because truth be told, most people love to be scared. Look at the person who drives on the beltway, an excellent example of someone with a death wish who is seeking a thrilling experience. Also, consider people who like to view Elvis Presley movies--that's pretty scary. You know, Elvis never really had to do any actual singing. All he had to do was stand before an audience and move his mouth (and certain other portions of his anatomy), because the girls were screaming so loudly they wouldn't have known if he was singing or not. I prefer my musical entertainment calmer, more sedate and conservative, like Lady Gaga.

The hard-core thrill seeker loves movies about horror, gore, murder and mayhem. The more blood splattered around on screen, the better. However, some of the older black and white movies were made before people had any blood in them because you never see a drop of it. Freddie Kruger, Michael Myers and Alvin the Chipmunk are some of the modern-day perpetrators of violence on the screen. They have replaced the Frankensteins, the Draculas and the Wolfmen of old, and these pioneers of movie mayhem don't like it one little bit. Being replaced has worsened their dispositions which were already pretty horrible, so they have ended up as retired, embittered old codgers living on pensions, gone and forgotten.

Frankenstein now uses a cane, Dracula has lost all his teeth and the Wolfman went bald, all over. How sad, because there was a time when Frankenstein would have knocked Freddie Kruger's block off, and Dracula would have bitten Michael Myers on the neck and flown away so quickly it would have made his mask spin around. The Wolfman may have had a little trouble with Alvin, though. Alvin's shrill singing might have made him howl like a dog in pain.

Speaking of retired monsters, as ghosts get older their ability to scare people by going *bump* in the middle of the night diminishes. In fact, some of them reach the age when they're unable to stay up until midnight, so the best they can do is go *bump* in the afternoon.

Halloween is the best example of people loving to scare and to be scared. The price of candy and costumes is enough to scare anyone out of a year's growth. Some people have tried in recent years to discourage the observance of Halloween saying it has become too dangerous. But the candy and costume manufacturers say, "No, the kids may have to eat around some pins and needles stuck in their treats, but look at the fun they'll have. Besides, in spite of the number of people at risk in wars, you don't hear anyone trying to discourage war or calling it too dangerous. We love to go to war or bomb somebody every chance we get. Don't be a pooty parper."

Finally, chocolate candy is the best Halloween treat, and that's what I always look for in my trick-or-treat bag. However, because it rots your teeth and makes you fat, minor inconveniences, some people have begun giving healthy food as treats, like carrots, celery or cotton candy. I say pooh on that. I once tried giving apples and oranges to trick-or-treaters, but after dropping an orange into the bag of an adorable little blonde girl dressed as an angel, it broke through her bag spilling all of her treats onto the ground. With that, the adorable little angel looked up at me disdainfully and kicked me in the shin!

15 – SETTLE DOWN, AMERICA!

In the year 1,000 A.D., before Christopher Columbus had even thought about discovering America, there was a man named Leif Ericson who lived in Greenland. He thought it was too cold there and wondered why it was called *Greenland* since it was covered with ice. So he set out to find a new, warmer place to live. He sailed southward where he had heard that the sun was shining and bumped into a land which he called Newfoundland. Since he had just found it, this was a very appropriate name. Leif established a colony in Newfoundland which he called *Vinland* because there were a lot of *vins* there. This is an old Norse word meaning *vine*, it's just that somebody left off the final *e*, which we all know makes the middle vowel say its name.

These *vins* or *vines* turned out to be cucumbers, tomatoes, grapes and cantaloupe, so he was very content in his new home because Leif Ericson loved high tea with cucumber and tomato sandwiches, scones with clotted cream, then grapes and cantaloupe for dessert. Soon though, he realized that he was not the only person there. There were some locals there called *Inuits*, because nobody could think of a better name. They didn't appreciate his barging in and eating all their fruit, so they began sneaking out of their igloos at night and throwing snowballs at him. Also, Leif had noticed that it was almost as cold in Newfoundland as it was in Greenland, so he decided to go home. Leif Ericson's experience discouraged other Norsemen from going to the new land, and the Inuits felt sure they had ended a serious threat to their homeland, but little they knew what was to come in future years. Just in case, they kept an extra supply of snowballs in reserve.

Another attempt to establish a colony in the New World happened in 1585 when Sir Walter Raleigh of England left a small group of settlers on Roanoke Island, NC, with the promise to return some day. He had discovered this new weed called *tobacco*, and he was going to try to convince everyone in England that they should stick it in their mouths and set fire to it. Unfortunately, the settlers he left behind were surrounded by tribes of hostile Indians. The Indians didn't know they were hostile, in fact they didn't even know they were Indians because they didn't live in India. They had been given that name by Columbus a century earlier who had no idea where he was, so he pretended to be in India and called everybody *Indians.*

The settlers should have realized that something was wrong when they looked around. The Indian huts were all decorated with scalps and shrunken heads, and the natives looked at them hungrily while licking their chops, rubbing their tummies and saying "Yum, yum!" So when Raleigh returned a few years later, surprise,

surprise, the settlers were all gone. Strangely, he didn't seem to understand why, even though the Indians seemed a bit chubbier and burped a lot with toothpicks in their mouths. He must have been wacked out on some of those weeds he'd been smoking. Smoking and hostile Indians can be hazardous to your health.

Then in 1607, a group of 104 people left England for the new world and established Jamestown, VA, the first permanent settlement in America.   King James I was named after it. The settlers arrived in three ships, the Susan Constant, the Discovery and the Goodspeed. These ships were so small, not much larger than a row boat, that most of the people wouldn't fit in them and had to be dragged along behind, so when they reached America, there were only 38 of them left.

In order to manage the new colony and to maintain discipline, the colonists selected a man named *John Smith*, an obvious alias. His real name was Al Capone, and he organized a syndicate to run the colony with an iron hand. Captain Smith, as he preferred to be called because it made him sound important, was able to establish friendly relations with the Indians in the area by making them offers they couldn't refuse, such as, "If you ever want to see your children again, you'll help us out." The settlers hadn't brought much food with them, and they arrived after all the stores were closed, so the Indians helped them by bringing food and teaching them how to plant crops, tie their shoes and jump rope.

The Indians were led by Chief Powhatan, or "He Who Powders His Hat," who had a beautiful daughter by the name of Pokemontas, the former Miss Oyster Fritter. One of the settlers named John Rolfe, a rival mob chief of Smith, fell madly in love with her as did John Smith himself. When Rolfe heard that Smith was also interested in Pokemontas, he went to Chief Powhatan and arranged for the Indians to eliminate Smith.

Pokemontas liked John Smith because he could make balloon animals, so just as they were about to flatten his cranium, she stepped in to save him, and they clunked her on the noggin instead. Powhatan was so impressed with her sacrifice that he spared Smith. However, the blow to her coconut must have scrambled her brains because Pokemontas married John Rolfe instead, for better or worse (better for her, worse for him).

Smith threatened a *vendetta,* though Rolfe said he never wears them, and warned John Rolfe to get out of town because it wasn't big enough for both of them (a line which would be used in some of the later Western movies). So Rolfe and Pokemontas left Jamestown and sailed back to England. This story is true because John Smith went on to have similar adventures in other foreign lands and always managed to be saved by a beautiful princess. Would Al Capone lie?

16 – FROM WITCHES TO WHITNEY

A very curious and unexplainable chapter in American history occurred in Salem, MA, in 1692, years after the Pilgrim settlement at Plymouth Rock, which by the way, is documented in another chapter of this volume. It seems that a few young girls suddenly turned into witches and were scaring the bat wings out of everybody, and it wasn't even Halloween. They would hide in bushes and when people passed by would jump out and scream, "Yeeaahahaha," and cackle like witches. Some people thought they were crazy and not really witches, but others said, "Oh no, they were witches all right because they had long crooked noses, wore pointy black hats and were riding broomsticks."

It was easy to identify a witch back in those days. In addition to their customary attire, if someone looked at you funny or mumbled something inaudible, you knew right away that he or she was a witch. Also, if someone passed by your house and your pig suddenly died, that was undeniable proof that the person was a witch. Many people were arrested and put on trial for being witches, and they were subjected to rigorous tests to prove their guilt or innocence. Some were thrown into ponds. If they floated, that proved they were witches. If they drowned, then they were excused. Sometimes, they would be found not guilty if they could name the person responsible for *possessing* them and causing them to become witches. This was a clever and effective tactic used by the court to root out the real criminals and bring the responsible people to justice.

After 19 defendants were executed for being witches, including a dog and a cat, people got tired of all this witchcraft business. The media no longer featured such stories on the front pages or on TV. The stories were buried in the society section of the newspaper, and people's interest turned to other matters such as how the Jamaican bobsled team would fare in the Olympics. Besides, people had decided if someone wants to be a witch, that's their own personal business and of no concern to us.

When all the fervor died down, people became very bored and were falling asleep, so in 1734 Jonathan Edwards came along and thought it was time for a *Great Awakening,* so he woke everybody up by yelling, "The British are coming! The British are coming!" Some people said, "There goes the neighborhood!" Others realized that he was too early and the British weren't coming yet, so they yelled at him to shut up and go back to bed.

However, in 1775, the British really did come, and Paul Revere ran around telling everybody. He had seen a signal in the Leaning Tower of Pisa which said, "One if by land, two if by sea and three if by air." At first, he didn't see any signal, so he asked Debbie Boone, who was in charge of lanterns, "Why didn't you *light up my light?*" She replied, "Because a mouse peed on the matches, and I had to use powder and flint."

When the British really did come, everybody got excited and started having parades, marching around like soldiers and shooting each other. This continued for about seven years until they ran out of bullets and decided to quit. They went to Paris and signed a treaty which turned the war over to the French who then had a revolution, stormed the Bastille, whatever that is, and guillotined everyone who wasn't nailed down.

After we got rid of the British, we had our own country called *The United States of America*. The country was divided into two halves. The northern half was called *The North*, and the southern part was called *The South*. The North had all the major industries like steel, coal, automobiles and bubble gum cards, but all the South had was cotton and moonshine. The moonshine industry did fairly well because the government sent down people called *revenooers* to advise the moonshiners on the best way to run their stills. But it took a lot of corn to produce the moonshine, also called *corn liquor, white lightnin', mountain dew, and formaldehyde.* People wanted the corn for corn fritters and popcorn, so the government asked the moonshiners, "Would you please shut down your stills to conserve the corn?" And they said, "Certainly." Everything was hunky-dory.

Then one day Eli Whitney, who lived on a mountain said, "Look, we have all this cotton, and we can fill up only so many medicine bottles to make it difficult to get the medicine out, so why don't we make moonshine out of cotton and kill two birds with one rock?" So he invented the cotton gin which turned cotton into a very dry gin. As a result, the production of cotton went sky high as did the production of gin. Eli Whitney never profited from his cotton gin, however, because most of the farmers were tea totallers and totally tippled only tea...totally.

Eli saw another opportunity, however. Since there was no more moonshining, there was a lot of corn left over, so he cornered the corn market, ground the corn into meal and opened Eli's International House of Hushpuppies. He also had a lot of gin left over from his cotton gin which he slipped into his hushpuppy recipe making his customers very happy.

17 - THE WIZARD OF LOUISIANA[3]

When Thomas Jefferson became President, he thought the country was too small. After all, it only had a North and a South. He wanted to add a West, so he said to France, "How much do you want for the Louisiana Territory?" which stretched nearly to the Pacific Ocean. Well, sensing an easy mark since Jefferson was new on the job, France answered, "840 trillion dollars." Now, Jefferson was no dummy, wasn't born yesterday and was nobody's fool so he said, "Would you compromise at a dollar eighty?" and they said, "Sure." (This turned out to be a real bargain, for if you tried to buy Louisiana today it would cost at least a hundred dollars, and you wouldn't get anywhere near as much territory.) Spain was mad at this because they had also been trying to get Louisiana to satisfy their love of crawdads and jambalaya. They considered sending an armada until someone said, "Don't forget what happened the last time we did that," so they dropped the idea.

After Thomas Jefferson purchased the Louisiana Territory, he wanted someone to explore it to see what was there and to find the Northwest Passage which someone had misplaced. So he suggested a Lewis and Clark Expedition and was lucky enough to find two guys who just happened to be named Lewis and Clark to run it. Lewis' first name was Meriwether, but he seldom told anyone because they always laughed if he did. Clark called him *Meri* for short, but Lewis didn't like this and told him to stop it. He wouldn't stop, though, so Lewis started calling Clark *fart face*. As a result, they never spoke a word to each other on the entire journey.

They set out from St. Louis, Mo, in 1804 and encountered all sorts of wild creatures: prairie dogs, Mormons, the Lost Tribes of Israel and used car salesmen, not to mention buffaloes which I won't mention. Most of them were very tame because they had never seen humans before and would eat right out of your hand--except the used car salesmen who would eat your hand plus an arm and a leg.

Lewis and Clark also met a little Indian girl from Kansas named Sacapatatas who became their guide. One day, she was sitting around her wigwam keeping her wig warm, when a cyclone suddenly blew it away (the wigwam, not her wig) landing it right on top of Osama bin Laden, squashing him flat. It was a very heavy wigwam being made from the skin of a very heavy... elephant. (I promised I wouldn't mention buffaloes.) Sacapatatas was very sorry about that and was told, "Oh, don't worry about it. Nobody liked him anyway because he was mean, picked his nose and smelled bad. But now you have to watch out for his brother, Salami bin Laden, who is much worse than Osama was."

So Sacapatatas and her dog, Tutu, were very scared, but Lewis and Clark said, "Oh don't be afraid, we'll protect you." (They always spoke in unison.) "Here, wear these red, sparkly shoes so we can find you in the dark." She thanked them saying, "Oh good, because I was told that Salami bin Laden tortures people by sticking pins under their finger nails, stripping their skin off and setting their hair on fire." To which Lewis and Clark said, "Well, we really have to be moving along now, but thanks for stopping by."

Sacapatatas asked them where they were headed, so they explained that they were looking for the Northwest Passage, and she chirped, "Oh, I know where that is!" She told them she had landed in a magic kingdom called Lilliput inhabited by these tiny people no bigger than donut holes who talked in high squeaky voices. Their leader was a good witch named *Gulliver* who told her to take the Northwest Passage, a road paved with yellow bricks, to Seattle. There, she would find the Wizard of Louisiana who would grant her every wish. She suggested to Lewis and Clark that they accompany her and maybe the Wizard would tell them how to find the Pacific Ocean. They also had to take along her three friends whom she had met: Harpo, Chico and Groucho, a clumsy scarecrow who played the harp, a big iron guy who played the piano and a grumpy lion who played cornerback for Detroit. Lewis and Clark, though dubious, loved slapstick and said okay.

Also, in addition to Salami bin Laden, they now had to be on the lookout for lions and tigers and bears, oh my! But somehow they made it through. When they reached Seattle, they asked where they could find the Wizard of Louisiana and were taken to the Space Needle where he was hiding behind a big curtain. All of a sudden, he jumped out and it was Salma Hayek--I mean, Salami bin Laden who yelled, "Smile! You and your mangy mongrel are on Sneaky Camera!" Upon hearing that, Tutu sprang up and bit Salami on the behind who screamed, "Ow! Get this mutt offa me!" Lewis and Clark said, "Throw some water on him!" but Salami yelled, "No, no, I never take a bath without my rubber ducky!" and ran away with Tutu firmly latched on behind.

At that moment, Lewis and Clark awoke and realized it was all a dream. Just then, the phone rang and they were told, "President Jefferson is calling." With that, their hair stood on end, and they screamed, "Don't call us, we'll call you!"

18 – THE BRITISH ARE COMING! AGAIN!

One of the many great innovators in American history was a man named Robert Clermont who invented the steamboat. He had tried many professions in life including painting, ballet dancing, umpiring, professional wrestling, juggling, astronauting and crocheting before turning to inventing. Among his many attempts at inventing were the papier mache' airplane, a wheel with four sides to it and a submarine with holes in the bottom which would sink but wouldn't resurface. Another invention was a soft drink he called *6-Up,* a great idea that was just one number short of success.

Clermont offered his inventions to the United States who said, "No," to England who said, "No," to Russia who said, "Nyet," to Germany who said, "Nein," and finally to France who said, "Wee, wee," which Clermont thought meant *yes*, but they just had to go to the bathroom. He also offered them to Japan who said, "#@&*!," but their mouths kept moving after they talked which confused Clermont who could only say, "You do, and you'll clean it up!"

Finally, he hit upon an idea which he thought would bring him fame and fortune. He created a game for two teams in which one team hits a ball with a stick and runs around in a circle. The other team tries to catch the ball and throw it at the runner to knock him out. If they do, he is declared *out,* literally. If they miss and the runner completes the circle, one point is scored for that team. Each team is allowed three *outs* during each *at bat.* Every two *at bats* is called an *inning.* There are nine innings per game. People said it would never catch on because there were too many inns and outs. They suggested that he invent baseball instead.

By this time, Clermont thought his career was over, so he decided to return to the U.S. However, he didn't have money for passage, so he invented his own steamboat and chugged home. While chugging homeward, Clermont's steamboat, the Kon Tiki, accidentally bumped into the British ship RMS Lusitania and sank it. The British didn't like this, so they began stopping American ships at sea and demanding that the sailors on board come serve in the British Navy. They offered an extra measure of grog and a two-week, paid sea-voyage vacation, but the Americans preferred to stay where they were because they didn't speak British. However, the British wouldn't take *No* for an answer and forced the American sailors to join them. This made America very mad. Well, for a long time, Americans had missed fighting with the British, it was so much fun, so we declared the War of 1812, 1813, 1814 and 1815 on them.

Not much happened during the war except the Indians went on the warpath, we beat up the British on Lake Erie and tried to invade Canada, while the British burned Washington, DC. They tried to invade Baltimore, but there was a ball game going on at the time, and they couldn't find any place to park. Then Francis Scott Keyhole wrote *The Star Spangled Banner* so people would have something to sing before the game and strain their voices trying to hit that high note. During the seventh inning stretch, the British bombarded Fort McHenry, so people went out and got beer and popcorn to enjoy while they watched the fireworks.

Down in New Orleans, Andrew Jackson beat the snuff out of the British, but found out later that the Treaty of Gout ending the war had been signed before the battle. Jackson said, "Oops! My bad," but Americans thought it was a very clever strategy on his part and elected him President.

19 – DON'T STEP IN THAT!

One of the big things to affect American farmers over the years was agriculture, and there was a lot of it lying around. Everyone thought that farmers should get rid of it because people were always stepping in it, but farmers didn't have many good tools with which to do so. To plow their fields, they had to use big tree branches pulled by a horse or the farmer's wife. Occasionally, strange things happened. One hot summer day, the Farmer in the Dell was plowing in the corn field. The sun was so hot that the corn started to pop. Well, the horse thought it was snowing, so he lay down and froze to death. This made plowing a very slow process.

The plows made in those days were not very strong and would often break, no matter what material they were made from. If the tree branch was big enough not to break, it was too heavy for the horse or the farmer's wife to pull, so they began experimenting with other materials. First, they tried balsa wood. Well, that didn't work. Other materials they tried were tinfoil, Styrofoam, Nerf and plastic, but someone said, "You can't use plastic because it hasn't been invented yet!"

So finally, a man named John Doe and Company said, "Why don't we try steel!" Well, you would have thought he had said, "Why don't we plow in the nude," because everybody looked at him as if he had split an infinitive.

"What's steel?" they asked.

"Real hard iron," he replied.

"Where are we going to get it!?" they wondered.

He answered, "I know this guy in Bethlehem who has a whole lot of it."

They said, "Who, Jesus?"

He said, "Not that Bethlehem--Bethlehem, Pennsylvania."

"Oh," they said.

(BACKGROUND: Early steel manufacturing in the United States was promoted and financed by Andrew Carnegie, the well-known *philanthropist* or stamp collector. A coin collector is called a *numismatist* which sounds like a nasal spray. END OF BACKGROUND.)

So John Doe and Company built this new plow out of steel, and everybody was so happy that they shouted, "Hooray," jumped up and down and went out plowing everywhere. They were planting crops on all the farms, roads, parks, rivers, back yards, window sills, rooftops, Lithuania and even in Yankee Stadium until Babe Ruth told them to stop it. They were planting so many crops that they couldn't harvest them fast enough.

Well, this other guy named Cyprus McCormick had invented a new reaper a couple of years before, but people said, "What's a reaper?"

He answered, "It picks your crops."

But since there weren't enough crops to pick at that time, they joked, "Looks like you've invented a grim reaper. Ha! Ha! Ha!"

Well, the joke was on them because now there were enough crops thanks to John Doe and Company and his new steel plow. So the whole country spent the rest of the summer sowing and reaping.

Reapers cost a lot of money, so Old MacDonald cleverly planted jumping beans which would jump right off the vine when they were ripe, thus eliminating the need for a reaper.

Other farmers asked for his secret and he explained, "As ye sow, so shall ye reap."

They walked away shaking their heads and saying, "I didn't know he was so religious."

20 – DON'T FORGET TO REMEMBERTHE ALAMO!

Meanwhile, down in Texas there was this place called the Alamo, an old mission, where a whole bunch of men were hiding from the Mexicans. They were hiding because the Mexicans had bad breath from eating all those burritos, frijoles and enchihuahuas. They also burped a lot. The owner of the mission kept telling the men to leave but they wouldn't listen, so he called up Antonio Lopez Miguel de Consuelo Federico Ramirez San Francisco Alfredo de Santa Anna con Carne with Mustard. They called him Santa for short. The owner had heard that Santa liked to play soldier and might help him get rid of these interlopers. Santa didn't know what interlopers were, but he said he would come anyway.

The interlopers were being led by Colonel William Travis and included Davy, Davy Crockett, Jim Bowie Knife and Harold the one-armed paper hanger.

When Travis was told that Santa was coming he exclaimed, "Oh boy! Let's put up the tree and get to bed early!"

But when they explained that it was the one with the army, he said, "What are the odds?"

They told him 5,000 to 1.

After they revived him, he cried, "We'd better send for reinforcements!"

They said, "You think?"

Unfortunately, the reinforcements never arrived in time, so Santa had this guy named Joshua blow his kazoo so loud that the Alamo fell down. This made Texas so mad that they said, "Just for that, you can't come to the Super Bowl!" Texas would later become the largest state in the union, including Jimmy Hoffa.

When the Alamo fell, it made a lot of noise and everybody in the country wondered what it was, but it was difficult in those days to communicate with people in other states, no matter how loud they shouted. So in 1844, a man named Samuel F. B. R. S. V. P. Morse invented the computer. No, that's wrong. He invented the telegraph and a bunch of dots and dashes which people could send to each other. Instead of saying, "Hello, how are you today," they could simply say, "Dot-dot-dash-dash-dash-dot-dash-dash-dot." And the other person would answer, "Dash-dot-dot-dash-dot-dash-dot-dot-dash." Nobody knew what the heck anybody else was saying, so Samuel F. B. R. S. V. P. Morse decided that he'd better add meaning to all the dots and dashes. Then people liked the telegraph much better. Somebody said, "Wouldn't it be easier just to use the telephone?" but was told, "No, because the telephone hasn't been invented yet."

Prior to the invention of the telegraph, people had to use the Pony Express to deliver messages. This was a system of horses and riders who would carry messages sewn in their underwear (the riders, not the horses) between St. Joseph, MO, and Sacramento, CA. Other parts of the country must not have had any horses because they didn't do it, so it was a very limited service. If you didn't live in St. Joseph or Sacramento, you couldn't send any messages unless you carried them yourself. Benjamin Franklin hadn't yet invented the post office.

The memory of the Alamo still lingered in people's minds. A lot of people were going around and shouting, "Remember the Alamo!" Some people had forgotten the Alamo but were afraid to admit it, so when people shouted at them "Remember the Alamo," they would say, "Yeah boy, you bet. Keep my ride alive!" just to make it sound as if they knew what was going on.

Then in 1846, to refresh everyone's memory, we declared war on Mexico, but nobody knew why. A lot of famous people were involved in the war: Errol Flynn, Rod Cameron, Randolph Scott and his uncle, big fat

General Winfield Scott played by Sydney Greenstreet. Even Ulysses S. Grant and Robert E. Lee fought side by side against the common foe. They became very close friends and vowed never to become enemies or fight on opposite sides. They continued to exchange Valentine cards right up until *you know what.* So much for vows.

When our soldiers invaded Mexico, they were told not to drink the water because it would give them hiccups. However, this became very difficult because once you bit into one of those tortillas loaded with jalapenos and habaneras, you had to drink something, quickly! In addition, it was too hot in Mexico and there were too many tourists, so the Americans wanted to leave. President Polk offered the Mexican President, Guadalupe Hidalgo, a peace treaty to end the war, and he said okay. Under the terms of the treaty, Mexico had to give the United States half of their country, all the territory that would become the States of Texas, California, Colorado, Nevada, Utah, Arizona , New Mexico, Argentina, New England, Florida, Bulgaria, Cuba and Gadsden.

It was a good thing we got California when we did because the very next year somebody discovered something there that would throw the entire country into a feverish frenzy. Marilyn Monroe! Not only that, they found GOLD! Everybody rushed to California and were called the Forty-Niners, as well as the Green Bay

Packers and the Baltimore Colts who were living in Indianapolis.

21 – THE UNCIVIL WAR AND WESTWARD O HO!

Along about the year 1861, the North and the South had become jealous of each other and decided to have a Civil War, though there was nothing civil about it. They started yelling at each other, throwing rocks and calling each other names like *Yankee Nasty Face* and *Rebel Stink Pot.* What started it all was, these two guys named Perry Mason and Richard Nixon drew a line in the sand they called the Mason-Nixon Line. They said that nobody could cross the line without giving the secret password. In fact, it was so secret they never told anybody what it was.

Well, General Robert E. Lee didn't listen, and took a Rebel Stink Pot army to Gettysburg, PA, where he had heard there were some Yankee Nasty Faces hiding. This made President Abraham Lincoln so mad that he went to Gettysburg himself and uttered those now-famous words, up on Big Top Mountain, "Hey, I can almost see my house from here!" He then suspended the writ of Hallelujah Chorus and hired General Ulysses S. Grant to go beat up Lee who ran away. Somebody said, "You shouldn't let Grant do that because he drinks too much." Lincoln replied, "Find out what he drinks, and give me the same thing."

After running around for four years, hiding and shooting at each other, Grant finally cornered Lee at Acrobatics Court House, where he put Lee on trial. The judge said that Lee was guilty and had to give Grant his sword plus walk a tightrope over a lake of alligators. This put an effective end to the war and everybody went back to what they were doing before.

One of the things they were doing before was trying to build a transcontinental railroad across the Pacific Ocean to connect the two continents, Asia and America. After several attempts during which the spikes wouldn't hold and the rails kept sinking, Abraham Lincoln said, "No, no! I said TO the Pacific, not THROUGH the Pacific!" They said, "Well, what are we gonna do with all these water wings?" Lincoln answered, "Put 'em on Craig's List."

They had hired all these Chinese workers to build the railroad thinking that they would be enthusiastic about building a railroad to China so they could all go home. They were called *Coolies* because they wore these cool-looking, wide-brimmed hats. The Chinese weren't discouraged by the change in plans, however, and agreed to continue working on the railroad because they knew that someday someone would invent an airplane, and they could then fly home.

Various routes were proposed for the new railroad. Some wanted to go through Canada, but the

Canadians said, "No way, Jose'" They thought we were Mexicans; they've never accepted the fact that the upstart United States is now to their south. So that gave others the idea of going through Mexico, but the Mexicans said, "We don't need no stinking choo-choo!" The Mexicans thought everything stunk. A guy from the Lionel Corp. said, "Why don't we just erect a giant Christmas tree in the middle of the country and have the railroad go around it in a circle?" They locked him in a room.

Other proposals would have taken the railroad through Maine or Florida, but Abraham Lincoln said, "Look, if we want to reach the Pacific Coast, then we should build in that general direction." So the directors of the railroad got together, held several committee meetings and concluded that the President was probably right. After they agreed in which direction they should go, they decided that the Union Pacific Railroad would begin building westward from Council Bluffs, IA, and the Central Pacific would build eastward from Sacramento, CA, and if lucky, they would meet somewhere out West. So they began in 1863.

Along the way, they encountered many steep mountains through which they had to dig. Picks and shovels were too slow, so they ran at the mountain really hard with their shoulders. That didn't work, but it sure did hurt. Then the Coolies tried digging through with their chopsticks which also didn't work. As a last resort, they switched to a new device called TNT (Thermo-Nuclear Timebomb), the most powerful explosive in the world.   However, nobody knew just how much of the stuff to use. The recommended dosage to blow a hole in a mountain was 1 ounce, but someone had lost the directions so they used a whole gallon. You know Mount St. Helen's in Washington State? Well, it used to be located in Nevada, but when they set off the TNT, it blew the entire mountain into Washington where it remains today, still smoldering.

Finally, after six years of arduous labor, the two railroads met at Promontory Summit, Utah, where they were going to join the lines together with a golden spike. Imagine their shock and dismay when they discovered that the Union Pacific had built their line in O scale, but the Central Pacific had used HO! The Lionel guy said, "See, I told you."

22 – A MAN, A PLAN, A CANAL, A MASSAGE

The most robust, energetic and active President we've ever had was Theodore Roosevelt. Teddy, as he was affectionately called, was named after the Teddy Bear which was popular at the time. He was a hardy outdoorsman through and through. He was always doing things outdoors like running, jumping, swimming, roller skating, bobbing for apples and horseback riding, especially horseback riding. It was hard getting him to come indoors to sign Presidential papers without his horse. Teddy especially liked charging his horse up hills. Show him a hill and he would charge up it whether it was a hill, mountain, butte, peak, cliff or speed bump. It didn't matter. He is best known for charging up San Juan Hill in Cuba. He also charged up all of Beverly's Hills in California and would have charged up Bunker Hill, but George Washington wouldn't let him.

One day while charging up Mount Vesuvius, he got the news that he had become President of the United States to which he said, "Bully!" He was always saying "Bully!" When he was awakened in the morning, called to supper or to the telephone, he would say, "Bully!" I've heard that this stems from when he was a boy and had a pet calf which he would carry out to the pasture every day. As the calf grew bigger and bigger, Teddy continued to carry it out to the pasture day after day, even after it became a full-grown, 1200-pound bull. And that's a lot of bull!

After he became President, it became necessary for him to go to Japan which was then located across the Pacific Ocean. At first, he wanted to ride his horse all the way, but when told his horse couldn't swim, he said, "Bully! I'll swim it myself!" Remember he was an avid outdoorsman full of vim and those other *v* words, and since the ocean was outdoors, it was perfectly logical to him. But his advisors told him he should take the transcontinental railroad to California and sail from there. Teddy didn't like this idea because there was no room on the train to ride his horse. He decided to take a boat from Washington and sail all the way around South America to Japan. He could then ride his horse around on the boat.

The journey around South America was a perilous one, fraught with dangerous storms, vampire bats, killer whales, palindromes and the deadly aurora australis. The southern tip of South America is called *Cape Horn* because of the big fog horn they keep there which can be heard all the way to Mt. Olympus. During the voyage, Teddy kept asking, "Are we there yet?" Finally, the ship captain got tired of this and said, "If you don't stop complaining, I'm gonna turn this boat right around and go home!"

Well, the voyage took about three months, give or take a month or two, and Teddy was very bored. When he got to Japan, he was so tired that he went and had a geisha foot massage where they walk around on your back. He enjoyed that so much that when he returned to Washington he said, "Bully! I want to do that again!" But it took too long to travel from Washington to Japan, so he suggested digging a canal right across America. He was assured that this was not feasible, and that a canal would have to be dug across the narrowest strip of land so he said, "How 'bout across Poland? Mongolia?" Teddy was not too sharp when it came to geography.

After an exhaustive study in which everybody went bug-eyed staring at maps, it was concluded that the most desirable place to build a canal would be across the Isthmus of Panama. Teddy said, "Bully," grabbed his shovel, headed for Panama and started digging.

At the time, Panama was controlled by Columbia who said, "Hey, you can't dig there!"

Teddy answered, "How 'bout if I pay you $25 million?" He was really eager to get that massage.

While Columbia was mulling it over and also thinking about it, Panama held a revolution, became an independent nation and said, "We'll take it!"

Teddy said, "Okay."

Columbia said, "Hey, no fair!" but it was too late.

Digging the canal took Teddy about 10 years, but it became one of the modern marvels of the world. Ships of all nations can now sail straight through Panama instead of taking the long and perilous route around Cape Horn. When he finished digging, Teddy was too tired to say *Bully*, so he said, "Whew! I need a massage."

23 – HOW CONGRESS WORKS

You probably don't know how Congress works. In fact, neither do I, but I've been watching it since it first began and have drawn some conclusions.

First of all, Congress was created way back in the Middle Ages when we were a very young country, so they can't be totally blamed for what happened. When our first Constitution was made, the country had just come through a very difficult revolution. So when our founding fathers and mothers were trying to come up with a governing body, the spirit of revolt was still in the air, and Congress was the most revolting body they could think of.

Congress is structured on the bi-cameral model, meaning two camels or a camel with two humps as opposed to the dromedary which is a cake mix. We got this model from England who have a Parliament with a House of Lords and a House of Peasants. The House of Lords is made up of rich, snooty landowners, and the House of Peasants is comprised of ordinary serfs who can't even speak Latin. They just hang around with nothing to do but smoke and watch the telly.

Our Congress is very similar. The Senate, called the Upper House because it's on the second floor of the

Capitol Building, is made up of Senators, two from each state, who are elected for six-year terms. Most people get tired of them before that, though, and wish they could throw them out of office, but it's too late. The 100 members of the Senate are presided over by the Vice President. This gives him something to do while he's waiting around for the President to kick the bucket. He is not allowed to vote, however, except in the event of a tie, so most of the time he just sits there sulking.

The Lower House on the first floor is called the House of Representatives and is full of people called Congressmen, or Congresswomen if they wear a dress. They serve two-year terms. The House, as it is called even though both the Senate and the House are *houses* of Congress, consists of 435 elected representatives of the people, but there aren't enough seats for all of them so some have to stand up. They are presided over by a Speaker of the House who seldom gets to speak because all the other members are always "yaying" and "naying." He has to bang the big hammer he keeps on his desk to get them to shut up. If you're not totally confused by now, stay tuned.

The number of Representatives from each state is dependent upon that state's population. Some states where not many people want to live, like Albania, have only one or two representatives, sometimes none if they're not really interested. Other states, like New York, California or Epcot, may elect 50 or more. This makes it very difficult to pass laws, however. Did you ever try to get 50 people to agree on anything? They can't even stay out of each other's way.

In the middle of the Capitol Building is the rotunda, a big round space with a high dome over it. The dome is so high that sometimes it will be sun shiny at the top but rainy down on the floor. As a result, the inhabitants walk around in a fog most of the time. They like to have fun by standing in the rotunda and shouting, "We're number one!" which creates a terrific echo. Try it the next time you're there. It's especially funny to do it with an Arabic accent and watch the reaction of the security guards who will then give you a guided tour of the basement. This is where they keep the dungeon with its iron maiden and water boards.

We have three branches of government: the Executive, the Legislative and the Judgmental. It is the function of Congress to serve as the legislative branch. In other words, they are the legislature which legislates by legislating legislative legislation. It is the duty of the Executive branch to execute any people who violate this legislation if the Judgmental branch says it's okay. Sometimes the Judgmental branch is hesitant to say okay because some judges don't want to be too judgmental.

The way Congress legislates is by having each member propose those bills which he or she feels would be beneficial to themselves, and if they also benefit their constituents, they try to do better next time. A member of Congress will propose a bill which is then passed on to a committee which argues about it for weeks and weeks before sending it to the full House or Senate where it is then argued over even more. Any legislation approved in the House of Representatives must then be passed on to the Senate and veesy vicey, where it is then argued over again before final passage. By this time, most members have lost interest and are reading comic books. If unapproved, the bill must then go back to where it came from, and the proponent gets whacked over the head with it for wasting everyone's time.

It is the duty of every Republican and Democrat in Congress to oppose any legislation proposed by the other party. If it comes from a Republican, every Democrat is sworn to vote against it. If a Democrat proposes it, the Republicans must do the same thing. One time a bill came forward and no one knew which party had proposed it. They became so confused that all their eyes glazed over, they wet their pants and sat there staring into space not knowing what to do. The bill died for lack of action, and Congress had to shut down for two weeks to recover.

Quite often, one party dislikes a proposed bill so much that it will do what they call *filibuster* hoping the proposing party will get so bored that it gives up. They do this by taking turns getting up and talking about anything and everything other than the proposed legislation. Sometimes they will simply read the Constitution, the complete works of Shakespeare or the Encyclopedia Britannica. Once in a while they will put on a magic show, do a song and dance or form a musical group and sing an opera. Although very entertaining, everybody eventually gets tired of this and will make them quit by voting *cloture*. This takes a majority vote equal to the square root of the hypotenuse of an irregular triangle when one of its legs are both the same. When they do this, it means that everybody has to sit down and shut up so they can get back to the business of running the country into the ground.

In order to keep themselves informed on upcoming legislation, members of Congress go off on what they call a *junket*. It's pretty much what it sounds like. They go off at taxpayer expense to remote parts of the world to educate themselves on the issues of the day. For example, if they want to learn more about snow-removal techniques, they go to Tahiti. To study how to properly cultivate and grow oranges, they visit Siberia. And a cruise of the Mediterranean to Greece is essential to develop a knowledge of plumbing and sanitation.

Once bills are approved by the House and Senate, they are then passed on to the President of the United States for approval or veto. If he approves them, he holds a big ceremony where all the big wigs from Congress and other freeloaders gather behind him. They all get their picture taken making faces and giving the President rabbit ears while he signs the bill into law. When signing, he uses many different pens and pencils which he then gives away to his friends and family as Christmas presents. Sometimes he will sign his name ten or twenty times just to get enough pens and pencils to give away--one of the perks of being President.

On the other hand, if the President does not like a particular bill, he will veto it. He does this by spitting on it, tearing it to shreds and stomping it on the floor. If the President vetoes any proposed legislation, it makes Congress very angry, and sometimes they will try to override the veto by yelling at the President and telling him if he doesn't pass it, they will hold their breath until he turns blue. (They don't seem to have quite grasped the concept.) This takes a $6\frac{3}{4}$ majority vote of all members with a shoe size over 11.

Whenever a Congress person's term is about to expire, he or she must campaign to be re-elected. This is called *stumping* for votes. It's called stumping because once the candidate begins speaking, the electorate is completely *stumped* as to what the heck he or she is talking about.

One way that Congress people get elected is by Gerrymandering. This is a system whereby they twist their voting districts all out of shape until they look like a person's digestive tract. This is why people in Congress are sometimes said to have a lot of *gastrointestinal fortitude*. They sometimes have to borrow territory from neighboring states to do this. The one who makes the most creative design is proclaimed the winner.

Congress doesn't meet all year round, only on special occasions, like during the third full moon of a month or when the Cleveland Browns go to the Super Bowl. Their Christmas vacation lasts until April 15 when they return to count all the income tax money and split it up between them. If there's any left over, they pay any outstanding bills. They stay in session until May 1 when they take their summer vacation, but they have to be back by November 1 in time to start their Christmas vacation again.

The President is always trying to get Congress to balance the budget, but it's so thick, sometimes consisting of 100 volumes of 1,000 pages each, that they couldn't balance it even if they used a sumo wrestler as a counterweight. Balancing the budget means not spending more than we earn. When we do, it's called *deficit spending* which is very bad. Right now, we have a budget deficit of over 16 trillion dollars. No, that's the truth. To eliminate this deficit, Congress would have to cut their salaries, benefits and perks almost in half, and since they set their own salaries, benefits and perks, the chance of this happening is the same as all of us becoming astronauts and flying to Saturn. Congressmen and women sometimes go there on a junket.

The trade deficit is another problem with which Congress pretends to be concerned. This is where we import more than we export which means, of course, that more money leaves the country than comes in. But since we love foreign products like French wine, Swiss cheese, German chocolate cake, Polish sausage, Canadian bacon, Brazil nuts, Indian blankets, Eskimo pies, pizza, spaghetti, Salma Hayek and Chinese fortune cookies, it's hard to keep up. About the only things we export are tobacco and artificial sweetener.

Every few months, the country runs out of money, and Congress has to approve new funding in order to keep the country running. Some people in Congress believe that this is their finest hour. According to the law, whenever we run out of money all Federal operations have to stop, and people are laid off from work...with one glaring exception: Congress is allowed to remain on the job! Well, they have to in order to come up with the dramatic eleventh-hour, bi-partisan funding agreement which will save the country and make them look like heroes. Many observers believe that they actually look like the eastern end of a herd of westbound horses.

Occasionally, Congress will invite the President to come over and give them a State of the Union address in which he tells them how the country's doing, as if they couldn't find out by reading the National Enquirer or watching CNN. When he comes, it's a big occasion. He arrives at the front door, but they won't let him in until they frisk him and validate his parking ticket. Then the guy who guards the door, I think he's called the Congressional Yeller, shouts, "Mr. Speaker, here he comes!" and shoves the President into the room. Then everybody stands up and starts yelling at the tops of their voices, laughing and clapping, throwing each other into the air and creating general mayhem until the President reaches the podium. This may take as long as an hour and a half because he has to shake hands with every member of Congress, their wives, husbands, mistresses, secretaries, reporters, page boys and people who just wandered in off the street to see what all the hub-bub was about.

Eventually, he reaches the podium and hands the Speaker and the Vice President envelopes containing his speech which they've already read because it was leaked to the media two weeks before. The Speaker then bangs his big hammer to make everybody shut up and has the audacity to say, "Ladies and Gentlemen I'm tickled pink, thrilled to my toes and pleased as punch to introduce to you the President of the United States." When he says this, it starts the whole melee all over again, and people clap, yell, scream and stomp their feet for another twenty minutes. He should just keep quiet.

When they finally do calm down, the President begins his speech. During the speech, it is mandatory that members of his party cheer and clap every time he says something, whether they understand it or not. The opposition party is supposed to sit on their hands and look constipated. Sometimes he will introduce someone in the balcony who has done something heroic, like the guy whose dog and mother-in-law fell in the river, but he saved the dog. When the President does that, everybody is allowed to cheer while the person being honored stands, waves and tries to look humble.

After the President's speech, which lasts about seven hours, everybody wakes up and holds a news conference. Those of the President's party will explain how good the speech was, but the opposition will tell us how bad it was. Then they all hug, kiss and make up and gather around the big pork barrel they keep in the middle of the room for barbecue sandwiches, pizza and light beer.

24 – THE PHONE, THE LIGHT AND THE FLAUT

Among the most important technological developments of the nineteenth century are the telephone and the light bulb. The first was invented by a man named Alexander Graham Bell who also invented the door bell, after which he was named—his friends called him *Ding-Dong*. His middle name indicates that he may be the one who invented the Graham Cracker as well. Since the Graham cracker is so dry, you have to eat it with a whole lotta milk to make it go down. Maybe that's why Alex invented the telephone; it gave people something to do while they wait on hold for their Graham crackers to get soggy enough to swallow.

I wonder if he used the phone to call people to convince them to buy his crackers; if so, Alexander Graham Bell was the first telemarketer. Wow! Telephone, door bell, telemarketer. He didn't want anyone to have a moment's peace! Just think, without him we would have been so bored with all the quiet time, we would have had to...I don't know...maybe like... read a book...while we eat Graham crackers.

Actually, the idea for the telephone was inspired by Prunella Ramshackle. She was the neighborhood gossip who thought she knew everything about everything and could spread gossip faster than Bertha Widebottom can polish off a dozen donuts. First there were drums, then smoke signals, the pony express, the telegraph and finally, Prunella Ramshackle. She would accost anyone who couldn't hide fast enough and encumber them with her take on the latest gossip. Alexander Graham Bell was often her primary target, and he wished there was some way to shut her up. So he invented the telephone, and she was ecstatic. Now she didn't even have to leave her house to annoy everyone. She could just call them up. This was just as Ding-Dong had planned it because now, instead of being bored to death by her endless prattling, he could just hang up on her. He especially enjoyed disguising his voice when she called and pretending to be his butler, Howe Long: "So solly. Missa Bell, he no here--he go to China," Howe Long is a Chinaman. Sometimes, he would simply hold his nose and imitate a busy signal.

The telephone was invented under nearly-tragic circumstances. One day while trying to concoct one of Little Sara's delicious recipes for hot cross buns, Alexander Graham Bell spilled battery acid in his lap. His reaction was rather swift and he yelled into the phone, "Holy S---! Watson com'ere quick!" Dr. Watson, who was Bell's assistant before teaming with Sherlock Holmes, was in the next room but was on the phone trying to avoid responsibility in a malpractice suit, so Alexander Graham Bell heard only a busy signal. The operator suggested, "Have a brandy, Alexander," which calmed him, but he never walked quite the same after that.

You may think that the invention of the telephone in 1876 followed closely by the electric light bulb in 1879 was rather coincidental. Actually, it was planned that way. In addition to being installed in private homes, the new telephones were placed in what were called public telephone booths, tiny little compartments with folding doors on them. When you squeezed into the telephone booth to make a call and closed the folding doors, a little light would come on above your head so you could see well enough to dial the phone and read your numbers to your bookie. Without the light, you might stick your finger up your nose, so it was necessary that they be invented together.

Superman used to rush to the nearest telephone booth to change clothes in an emergency, but since not many of them exist anymore, he now has to drag one around with him wherever he goes, just in case. He once used one of those little photo booths to change clothes, but the camera went off unexpectedly and the resulting pictures were published on YouTube. He never did that again. J'ever notice that each of the super heroes has his gimmick? Superman has his phone booth, Batman has his Batmobile ("Holy gas guzzler, Batman!"), Captain Marvel says, "Shazam!" and as everyone knows, The Incredible Hulk plays the flute.

For some reason, a flute player is called a *flautist.* Why? A clarinet player is called a *clarinetist,* a trombone player is called a *trombonist,* so it seems that a flute player should be called a *flutist.* On the other hand, a trumpet player is a *trumpeter* and a fiddle player is a *fiddler,* so maybe it should be *fluter.* Of course, if we change the name of the instrument to the *flaut,* problem solved. That brings to mind what to call a tuba player? Sorry, I hope you won't lose any sleep tonight pondering that question. By now, you probably think I've forgotten my topic, but I wrote it down in my opening paragraph just in case. Uhh...

To shed a little light on the topic, the light bulb was invented by Thomas Alfalfa Edison who also invented the stock ticker which caused people to jump out of their windows following the stock market crash in 1929. That's right. If there were no stock tickers, no one would have known how badly their stocks were doing and wouldn't have jumped: cause and effect. When someone came up with the glow stick, thinking it would replace the light bulb, Thomas Alfalfa Edison jumped out of his window. Fortunately, it was on the ground floor, so he was okay. As it turned out, the glow stick was a fluke anyway. Is someone who uses a fluke called a *flaukist,* a *flukist* or a *fluker?*

25 – THE COLD WAR

The Cold War began in the winter of 1945 following a very hot war called World War II. People had gotten tired of hot war and wanted a change of climate. So, instead of hurling bombs, rockets and bullets at each other, they just threw icy stares, frosty comments and cold shoulders. Now you know why it was called the *Cold War*. This would last until the late 1980's when the Berlin wall fell down right on top of the Soviet Union causing it to also collapse. The Soviet Union had been composed of all those Communist countries like Russia, Afghanistan, Uzbekistan, Snowballstan and all the other *stans*.

Following the War, Germany had been divided between the good guys, Americans, English and French (Yay!), and the bad guys, the Soviets (Boo!). And in a mind-boggling strategy, the capital of Germany (Berlin) was placed entirely within the Soviet zone which, of course, meant that they could block access to it any time they wanted. They tried it once, but we broke the blockade by flying airplanes into Berlin filled with all the necessities of life: coffee, bubble gum and Playboy magazines.

Berlin itself was also divided between East and West, but so many people escaped into the West every day that East Berlin was looking as devastated as Macy's toy department following a pre-Christmas sale. Well, the Soviets wouldn't stand for this, so they said, "Lachanya nitshchki" which means, "We won't stand for this," and they built a high, high wall all the way across Berlin to keep people from escaping. This prompted President Kennedy to go there and proclaim to everyone, "Ich bin ein Berliner!" which means, "I am a jelly donut!" I wonder why the East Berliners didn't just walk around the wall.

When President Kennedy was inaugurated in 1961, he told Americans, "Ask not and don't tell!" And they didn't. He was known for saying famous things like, "I will go to the moon by the end of this decade." He didn't but we did, and you can read about it in another chapter of this volume, *The Story of Flight, Part 2.*

Most of the credit for bringing down the Berlin Wall should go to President Ronald Reagan because he went there and said, "Mr. Gorbachev (who was in charge of the wall at the time), tear down this wall!" and it immediately fell down! Everybody wondered why he hadn't said something sooner.

He and Premier Mikhail Gorbachev of the Soviet Union had previously met in (Rakelvink, Rakyavitch, Raykavitski?) somewhere in Iceland (remember it was the Cold War) and agreed to disagree. They had met to discuss SALT because the Soviets needed a lot of it to melt all the snow in their streets, but Reagan *peppered* their SALT (Heh! Heh!) by proposing that they make a movie sequel to *Star Wars* so he could play Yoda. He had been a movie star before being infected with politics and yearned to be one again. Gorbachev wanted to play Princess Leia, but Reagan insisted he play Jabba the Hut. Alas, they never came to terms, so Jabba ended up playing himself.

See, that was the nature of the Cold War, no actual fighting, just a lot of disagreeing. For example, earlier Vice President Richard Nixon had an argument with Soviet Premier Nikita Khrushchev in a Moscow kitchen. They both insisted that they could make a better chicken soup than the other. Khrushchev had previously sought help from Cuban Leader Fidel Castro at the United Nations where Khrushchev had gone to bang his shoe on the table. He was full of class and style. Castro had brought live chickens to put in the soup, but both he and Khrushchev were made to leave because Nikita had stinky feet.

During the Cold War, the United States had all these huge B52 bombers flying around which carried a million billion tons of nuclear bombs. They were in the air all the time just in case somebody started something. As a joke, we would fly them toward the Soviet Union making it look like we were attacking, then at the last moment the planes would veer off and go back. By then, though, the Soviets had gone to

DEFCON 4 and prepared to launch their nuclear missiles, but we said, "Ha! Ha! Made you look!" and everybody had a big laugh. It was very funny and helped relieve the tension during the Cold War.

Another incident that occurred during the Cold War which nearly caused another hot war was the Cuban Missile Crisis. President Kennedy was flying his U2 spy plane over Cuba one day and discovered that the Soviets had placed ICBM's (In Credibly Big Missiles) there in an attempt to threaten the U.S. in the same way that we had missiles placed all around the Soviet Union.

Well, the President was incensed. He yelled at them, "You can't do that because it's against the Monroe Doctrine!"

The Soviets yelled back, "Well you did it to us!"

He replied, "Too bad! You don't have a Monroe Doctrine, and we thought of it first! So there!"

He demanded that they remove all the missiles or he would invade the Bay of Pigs. His advisors told him, "We already tried that, and all we found were some surprised sunbathers and a bunch of pigs." Finally, though, the Soviets relented and removed the missiles, but only after we agreed to let Premier Khrushchev visit Disneyland.

In an earlier incident, the Russians had accidentally shot down a U2 spy plane which was flying over the Soviet Union taking pictures for travel brochures. They had captured the pilot, Francis Gary Powers, but agreed to trade him back for a Mickey Mantle rookie baseball card. We said, "Throw in a case of vodka, and it's yours," which they did. Francis Gary Powers would later go on to fame by changing his name to Bono and forming a famous rock group named after his plane.

Now, thank goodness, the Cold War is over! Gone are the days when both sides would threaten each other and pretend they were going to blow the other one all to Hades. Nowadays, if there is a disagreement anywhere in the world, we actually go there and start bombing everybody. There's no confusion as to where we stand. We're for truth, justice and the American way, and we won't be terrorized by some foreign power bullying us and trying to shove us around. It's a wonderful feeling to live in a stable, civilized world of peace, harmony and tranquility backed up by strong, decisive action.

26 – WATCH YOUR LANGUAGE!

Language is something we use when we want to talk to each other. Sometimes. We don't use it as much as we used to prior to the advent of television. Language was invented a long, long time ago when God built the Tower of Balderdash and taught everybody how to speak different languages. At first, nobody knew how to talk, just like babies. J'ever wonder how babies think? I mean, they don't know how to talk, but they must have thoughts. Maybe they see subtitles or cue cards. I don't know.

People used to talk in a similar way before the invention of language. They would just hold up pictures of what they wanted to say. For example, if they were hungry, they would hold up a picture of a banana.   If they were sleepy they would show a picture of a bed. If they wanted to propose marriage to someone, they would show a picture of Mickey Rooney. Those were the three basic needs in life, even with animals: the need to eat, sleep and prevaricate, I mean procrastinate, no I mean procreate. Life was much simpler then.

Then, as life became more complicated, we needed more and more pictures. We needed to say things like, *Take me out to the ball game, Fly me to the moon* and *Are you gonna be in there all day?* We especially needed *I declare war*, a saying that was becoming ever more necessary as years went by. God decided it would be simpler if He just taught us how to talk, so He introduced the languages of Greek, Latin and Pig Latin.

Well, that was fine if you happened to be a Greek, a Latin or a pig, but many people weren't and demanded that God give them their own language as well, which He did. Eventually, there were hundreds of languages in the world and still are. Many of them evolved from these earlier languages, like French and Spanish which devolved from Latin. And coincidentally, people in France still speak French just as people in Spain still speak Spanish. Isn't that interesting? People in Mexico also speak Spanish, but at one time Mexico was inhabited by the Mayans who spoke Mayonnaise. People in the Swiss Alps speak very softly so they don't start an avalanche.

Sadly, nowhere on the scene could you find English! That's right. The English people kept asking God to give them a language, but God was reluctant to do so because He knew they would want to control the world someday and sing, "Rule, Britannia!" Instead, he invented German. However, nobody wanted to speak German. It started in northern Europe around Denmark, which someone cleverly named *Jutland* because it "juts out." But they didn't want it and shoved it down to southern Europe where it lay in state until the English people said, "Hey, what are you gonna do with that language lying there? If you don't want it, we'll take it." So the people of Europe got rid of it by passing it off to the Angles and Saxons when they migrated westward. They were so named because the Angles walked funny and the Saxons played horns.

After a while these Germanic speaking Angles and Saxons began moving across the English Channel which was then known as the Learning Channel. The land in which they settled became known as Angleland or England, and their language was called Anglo-Saxon or Old English as opposed to New English which was spoken by people in New England, but nobody could understand it. Many still can't. So the English then had their own language even though it originally started as German which nobody wanted.

German was not totally abandoned, however, because a few hardy stragglers who had developed a craving for sauerkraut und Wiener schnitzel stayed and founded the country of Germany. Somebody had to do it, and since they already had the language, they figured, "Why not?"

The English language evolved so much over the years that people today would not be able to understand a person speaking English about 1,000 years ago. Of course, sometimes we can't understand people using

English today, especially if they're screaming modern rock music, but that's another story.

Still, God didn't want the English to have their own language so He complicated it by making the language too difficult to spell. When asked how it should be spelled, God said, "*I* before *e*, except after *c*, unless pronounced *ay* as in *neighbor* and *weigh*." Then He tried to trick us by sneaking in words like *either, neither being seized weird, feisty foreigners,* and *heightened heifers heisted a leisurely, heigh-ho seismology*, all with e before *i*. You see any *c's* in these words?

And as if that weren't enough, He said that *bomb, comb* and *womb,* with identical endings, must be pronounced differently, as should *cove, love* and *move, give-dive, come-home, height-weight, great-wheat, lost-most, touch-vouch, choose-loose, sieve-grieve* and *frozen-dozen.* However, *choose, lose* and *booze,* spelled differently, will rhyme as will *frozen* and *chosen, dozen* and *cousin, room, tomb* and *whom, straight-freight, ream-seem, sieve-give* and *caught-fought.*

Then to top it off, He made us learn *ough,* the deadliest letter combination in any language, as in *though, through, thought, bough, enough* and *cough,* each pronounced differently. We could discuss other letter combinations, but it makes my head hurt so I'm going to stop--if I can--it's like eating potato chips.

Just pity the poor foreigner learning to pronounce all these words or the unfortunate fifth-grader studying them for a spelling test.

It's a wonder that the language even survived. In fact, if it hadn't been for this big rock that Napoleon found while he was in Egypt hunting Sphinx, it might not have. I think it's called the Rock of Gibraltar. On it were inscribed three unknown and indecipherable languages: Cockney, Southern U.S. and Brooklynese (*Ya heah dem boids choipin? You mean birds. Wull, dey soun' like boids.*), each one instructing the reader in the proper use of the sling shot. Napoleon went so wacky trying to read it that he turned his hat around sideways, stuck his hand in his coat and was taken away to a remote island. The rock was then taken over by the English who put it in the British Museum. They couldn't read it either.

Well, it turned out that God was right. As soon as the English learned to speak, they began building an empire which eventually stretched around the world. At one time, counting all the territories, colonies, dominions, states, protectorates, outposts, trading posts, fence posts, camel drivers, and lemonade stands, the British Empire comprised nearly 500 million people, about one-quarter of the earth's population. And yes, they began singing "Rule, Britannia!" What a racket!

In addition to Great Britain, which consisted of England, Scotland, Wales and Ireland (under protest), other major British possessions were Australia, Canada, India, New Zealand, Old Zealand, South Africa, Hong Kong, King Kong, Ping Pong, Piccadilly Circus and Trafalgar Square. They also owned water-front property in various other countries in Africa, Antarctica, Asia, Europe, North and South America and Jupiter. They once tried to keep the United States, but that didn't work out too well; in fact, many other former British possessions now belong to someone else. A famous writer once proclaimed, "The sun never sets on the British Empire!" but that British sun went down a long time ago.

And just think, it all started because we couldn't keep our mouths shut.

27 – THE AMERICAN PASTIME

No, America's pastime is not eating greasy foods and belching. Many long years ago, or to be specific, in 1800-something, some guy named Lil' Abner Doubleplay invented the fascinating game of *baseball*. Well, many people believe that Abner did not really invent the game, but only claimed to have done so to get in free. They say it actually was created by a man named Hector Hardball. He called it *baseball* because the name *chess* had already been used. He first wanted to name it after himself but was told that nobody would want to play a game called *Hector*. However, some people still refer to it as *hardball* just to honor Hector's memory.

It's referred to as America's pastime because a whole bunch of people in America *pass the time* (get it?) by watching, listening to or playing the game. Every young boy and many girls, at some time or other, play baseball. Many men continue to play into their adult years, and when they get older and develop beer bellies, they convert to *softball*, although if you've ever been hit by one it really isn't very soft (the ball, not the bellies). If some baseball players are very, very good at playing, they may enter what is called *professional baseball* where they can earn scads and scads of money, even more than the President of the United States. The President can't play baseball because the Secret

Service won't let him. Just as well, 'cause many people believe he doesn't know his elbow from first base anyway.

Being *very, very good* means a player must be able to hit the baseball hard and far, but not necessarily frequently, only about 3 out of 10 times. He must also be able to run fast without falling down and catch the ball and throw it without hurting himself or anyone else, very often. If he is able to run, field and hit well, he is known as a *triple threat.* The catcher is known as a *quadruple threat* because not only must he run, field and hit, he must be able to squat. He is the only player in any sport who squats while he plays. (I know what you're thinking, but a hockey goalie doesn't squat, he stoops.)

If a player becomes a pitcher, he is not expected to hit very well, but he must be able to throw the ball so hard that it makes a loud *pop* in the catcher's mitt. This is meant to scare the batter. The pitcher is the guy who *pitches* the ball, the catcher is the guy who *catches* it and the batter is the guy who *bats* or hits the ball before it hits him. If there is any confusion about these designations, please refer to the American Pastime Encyclopedia of Redundant Terminology, Section 8, Subsection "Duh!"

The game of baseball is played loosely along these lines: Each batter comes to home plate or the *dish* (a pentagonally-shaped white thing on the ground) where he's supposed to stand while the pitcher throws the ball at him. There is a prescribed ritual which the batter must complete before batting. He must adjust his cap, shirt, pants, socks and jock strap, scratch himself in important places, tighten his batting glove to keep his hands warm, spit on the ground to annoy the catcher (especially annoying with a wad of tobacco in his mouth), knock the dirt from his spikes (shoes with sharp, steel points underneath to disfigure the second baseman), then pound the plate and take several practice swings with his bat.

Before stepping up to the plate, he then glances at the third base coach who is suddenly seized with muscle spasms and starts flailing his arms about. After assuring himself that the coach is okay, the batter then turns to face the pitcher. The batter is expected to perform this ritual after every pitch. If he didn't, the game would be over in thirty or forty minutes and the spectators would feel that they hadn't gotten their money's worth.

The batter is allowed three swings of his bat in trying to hit the ball. If he misses all three times he is declared *out* and must return to the dugout where the rest of his team try to ignore him while he throws his bat and helmet, says a lot of very bad words and destroys the water cooler. Sometimes, the batter will not swing at a pitch in the hope that the pitcher will get tired and *float* one in there that the batter can really *crush* (technical baseball terms understood only by the true aficionado).

However, to neutralize this strategy which just delays the game, there is a man standing behind the catcher called the umpire who used to dress all in black even on hot, summer days. If he thinks that the batter should have swung at a pitch even though he didn't, the umpire is allowed to call the pitch a *strike*. When this happens, the batter will turn and glare at the umpire as if he is something that an animal left behind. And if the umpire yells, "Strike three," this makes the batter so angry that he throws his bat, his helmet, the umpire, the catcher and anything else he can get his hands on while expressing some very bad words even before he gets back to the dugout.

This behavior usually excites the fans (short for *fanatic raving maniacs*) so much that they will yell, "Kill the umpire!" and throw various hard objects onto the field in the umpire's general direction, such as batteries, beer bottles and stadium seats. Eventually, they calm down and another batter comes to the plate to start the whole process all over again.

Sometimes, a player will become so disruptive and throw such a tantrum that the umpire will eject him from the game so the fans won't have to watch such embarrassing antics. Occasionally, this makes the manager mad, and he will confront the umpire too, but the manager must be a short, stocky guy who has to stand on his tip toes until their noses meet. Sometimes he will kick dirt on the umpire's feet or question the umpire's lineage. When this happens, he may also be ejected because the umpire spent half an hour before the game polishing his shoes. In order to make them leave the field, all four umpires gather in a bunch so the batter and his manager will know that they are clearly outnumbered and had better not start anything.

This doesn't always work, however, because occasionally, both teams are allowed to pour onto the field to vote for whom they think is right. This usually happens whenever the batter gets hit with a pitched ball prompting him to approach the pitcher, bat in hand, to discuss his concerns with the pitcher. (Why anyone would throw anything at a guy holding a big stick, I don't know.)

Once they flood the field, the players gather in small groups and start yelling, shoving and rolling around on the ground. It's a lot of fun. This is called a *Donnybrook*, but I don't know why. I assume it was named after some guy named *Donny* who must have loved causing trouble. After the players finish voting by knocking each other around, they return to their dugouts and the game resumes.

In the event a batter doesn't swing at four pitches and none of them is called a *strike* by the umpire, the batter is allowed to *walk* to first base. Whenever a batter reaches first base, the first baseman will engage him in conversation, as if they are old friends, in an attempt to distract him so the pitcher can throw the ball at him and knock him out.

If the batter is pleased with the way the ball is pitched, he may try to hit it. If he hits it into the air, it may be caught by an opposing player, and if the ball is hit on the ground, a player may field it and throw it to first base before the batter arrives there. In either case the batter is *out* which causes him to kick the dirt and throw his helmet to the ground, but the opposing players are so happy that they play catch with each other before the next batter comes to the plate.

If the batter is fortunate enough to hit the ball where there is no fielder, one of four things can happen: he runs to first base, second base, third base or to home plate, depending on how long it takes the opposing players to find the ball and throw it at the batter who is now running around the bases. To avoid being hit, the batter tries to knock the ball out of the park for a *home run.* Then the opposing players can't throw the ball at him, and he is allowed to run home safely. After he returns to the dugout, his team mates welcome him by jumping on him, hitting him on the head, giving him high fives or fist bumps and spanking him on the butt.

Baseball is a man's sport. The team which administers the most high fives, fist bumps and butt spanks wins the game.

Some of the early professional baseball teams in America were the New York Knickerbockers, the Cincinnati Red Stockings and the Chicago Black Sox. The Knickerbockers used to wear knickers, you know those heavy corduroy pants which your mother made you wear to school and would *whiff* when you walked? The Red Stockings wore these red stocking caps which made them look like a bunch of Santa Clauses, so they stopped doing that and began wearing red socks instead. A team in Boston now does this as well.

The most notorious team of all time was the Chicago Black Sox. They became embroiled in a terrible scandal for laundering their socks so infrequently that they turned *black*! This is not surprising when you consider that some of their players, like *Shoeless* Joe Jackson, played in their stocking feet. What did they expect would happen? It is sad that some of the players involved in the scandal were barred from baseball for life by Judge Kenesaw Mountain Landis, the baseball commissioner at the time. With such an imposing name, no one dared disagree with him. The players begged forgiveness, but the Judge wouldn't change his mind even when *Shoeless* Joe promised to put his shoes back on.

Baseball is still a very popular sport, even though many fans feel that the players are being paid far too much money for simply playing a game every day. They feel that such high salaries should be paid only to those responsible people who actually earn them, like politicians and corporate executives.

28 – MY COMPUTER CRASHED WHEN I HIT IT WITH A HAMMER

There is an evil entity thriving in our midst today. Like an omnipotent being it calls us, tempts us, commands us and forces upon us its evil influence and domineering presence. Most of us have accepted it into our lives and have succumbed to its nearly-erotic attraction. No incubus or succubus has ever wielded such power. Daily, we respond to its controlling force like robots manipulated by a mad scientist. Many of us have formed an alliance with it and its demands on our time, talents and very existence. Oh, such is the devious nature of this evil being that we actually believe that it belongs, can be useful and should play a major role in our lives, not realizing that this belief is leading us down a path to oblivion from which we can never return. This evil entity that we have allowed to descend upon us like a shroud of death is *THE COMPUTER*!

My computer has always hated me! I've never felt that way about an electrical appliance before. My radio has always treated me kindly by providing music, drama, news and information at the push of a button or the twist of a dial, always under my control. Even my television has been a worthy companion most of the time, except in the early days of Mad Man Muntz when the vertical hold wouldn't hold. (Also, I would be remiss if I didn't mention that TV programming today is in the toilet.) Nevertheless, my radio and TV are my friends. Never once do I have to worry about them crashing or developing a disabling virus, for which there is no vaccine.

Then someone who shall remain blameless, because I don't know his or her name, invented *THE COMPUTER*! With that, my whole world changed. Thenceforth, I had to worry about junk mail, spam, scams, spyware, popups, viruses, whooping cough and pneumonia. I always had the feeling that I should take my computer to the vet periodically for shots. The computer has never been my friend.

People said, "The computer will give us access to the information highway; we'll have the internet and e-mail. We can learn everything we always wanted to know. We can communicate electronically with people." Didn't someone invent the telephone for that purpose? The computer could be a useful tool if it would perform its function without trying to dominate us. For example, have you ever gotten the message from your computer, "You do not have the authority to perform this action." What?! Whadda ya' mean, *I don't have the authority?!* It's my friggin' computer...I can do anything I want with it! To which the computer responds, "Byte me!"

Owning a computer means having to use e-mail, whether we want to or not because everyone else is using it. We must go to our computers several times a day to see if we have any messages, many of which turn out to be junk. And some people have the audacity to further annoy us by requiring that we acknowledge receipt of their junk before we can even open it! I wonder how they would react if we insisted that they acknowledge receipt of our acknowledgment.

That's bad enough, but now we're expected to join *Facebook* and beg people to be our friends and to tell them that we *like* the drivel they post on their pages. Well, maybe there are some people we don't want as friends, and maybe we don't like having to tell people what we like. There should be an option to indicate what we DON'T like. The computer has taken over our lives.

Not that I'm opposed to technological advancements. I do have a cell phone because it is expected, but so far, I've resisted the pressure to *text, tweet, tweedle, twitter, flitter, burp or toot.* Do we have to inform someone about our every conscious thought or action? ("Well, I'm walking down the street, now," or "Here I am in the bathroom.") Some of us may still have quiet, personal thoughts that we don't want to express to someone. ("I wonder how often Salma Hayek thinks of me.") I do not have an I-Phone, I-Pad, I-Pod, I-Patch, I-Sore, I-Swear and I-Don't expect to

I-Surrender to any of them anytime soon. I don't want a telephone that's *smarter* than I am, whether blackberry, blueberry, huckleberry or beriberi. Fruit belongs in a bowl, not on the telephone. But these annoyances I can handle; not the computer.

There it sat, every day, lurking, staring at me, just daring me to try using it, trying to lull me into a false sense of security by looking innocent. But I knew what it was thinking: "Just when he gets into the middle of typing a long document, I'm going to freeze up so he'll have to start all over. Ahahahaha!" It had pushed me too far--I had to take action.

It came down to a choice between me or it, and one of us had to go. Most of my family felt it should be the computer, and I agreed. So last night, when it wasn't looking, I sneaked up behind it with my little hammer and gave it forty *whacks* just like Lizzie Borden. Boy did it feel good! Talk about crashing! And now it's over--finally, I'm free! I have broken the bonds of slavery which have chained me to a life of obeisance and sycophancy. No more junk mail, no viruses, no Facebook, no pop-ups, no freezing, no games…Wait a minute! What was that? NO GAMES? Oh no, what have I done?!

A TRIP TO THE MOVIES!
(Bring your own popcorn.)

Many classic novels have been adapted to film over the years and have inspired the creation of other films of the same genre. I've enjoyed a number of these movies as I'm sure you have. The following are my versions of some of these classic tales. I hope you find them amusing, though you may not remember them in quite the same way.

29 – FAMOUS MONSTERS I HAVE KNOWN

The stories you are about to read are true. They were documented by Universal Pictures in several series of films they made during the 1930's and 40's. I know they're true because I saw these documentaries, and if you've seen it on the silver screen, you can take it to the bank!

FRANKENSTEIN[4]

The most famous of the famous monsters I have known is Frankenstein. You might call him, *The King of the Monsters,* but not to his face 'cause he'll knock your block off! *Frankenstein* is the story of a very lonely scientist who couldn't make any friends. He tried to make friends but could never seem to find the right words, "Good morning, you big, fat pig! Would you like to be my friend, you ugly, ignorant freak?!" People didn't warm to this approach, so one day, while tinkering with his chemistry set, he decided to create his own friend. The result was a big, dumb, butt-ugly brute who didn't know his own strength, and he wasn't very friendly.

Frankenstein was named after his creator who shall remain anonymous. He first named him *Arnold Hathaway* but realized that *Frankenstein* sounded scarier and was more marketable at Halloween. He was so ugly that whenever he entered a room, people would scream and faint. This annoyed Frankenstein to no end, so he knocked their blocks off. This made him very unpopular, and he began receiving fewer and fewer party invitations. One day his creator said to him, "Frankenstein, you really shouldn't be knocking people's blocks off because it disorients them severely." So Frankenstein proceeded to disorient him right into the middle of next week.

At 9' 3½" tall, Frankenstein was one of the tallest monsters on record. Godzilla comes to mind, but he doesn't count because he was in those Japanese movies where the actions don't match the words. They yell, "Godzilla!" and their mouths continue to move for 12 more seconds. It's like watching a movie with the wrong sound track attached. True, much of Frankenstein's height can be attributed to the 12" high, Dr. Love boots he wears, still the L. A. Dribblers invited him to try out for their team. Unfortunately, Frankenstein's creator had forgotten to put any hinges in his knees, so he walked very stiff-legged. Running was next to impossible, so by the time he reached one end of the basketball court, all the other players were back at the other end. So he knocked their blocks off.

After a while, people got tired of all this block knocking off, so they organized themselves into unruly mobs, wearing lederhosen and knee-high socks with little feathers in their hats while yodeling. They carried torches, clubs and pitchforks. They would have brought rockets, bombs and flamethrowers with which one normally fights monsters, but the burgomaster owned the torch, club and pitchfork concession in town, and business was slow.

The burgomaster urged them onward, "Even though he's bigger, more powerful and may rip you all to shreds, you must get him! I'll wait here. O-de-lay-dee-hoo!" However, he should have known that you can't destroy Frankenstein. No matter how many times he was set on fire, frozen in ice or thrown into quicksand, he always came back in the next movie perfectly whole and stronger than ever.

Some of the documentaries made about him are entitled, *Frankenstein, The Bride of Frankenstein, The Son of Frankenstein, Frankenstein's Mother-in-Law* and *Frankenstein's Second Cousin, Once Removed.* The closest they came to defeating him was when he met Abbott and Costello who made him laugh so hard that he wet his pants and had to run, or stiff-leg, away. So, if you ever meet him in a dark alley, which is where you would normally meet a monster, be sure to tell him some jokes, and maybe he won't knock your block off.

COUNT DRACULA[5]

The weirdest of the famous monsters I have known has got to be Count Dracula. He's the one with the long fangs in front with which he bites people's necks and sucks their blood. Eww! And boy could he polish off an ear of corn!

He would paint his face white and always wore a tuxedo, a long black cape with a red lining and one of those silk top hats; you know the kind which you could mash flat but always popped back into shape when you wanted to wear it again? Remember in some of the old movies when people would sit on one of those hats and the audience thought it was crushed and laughed out loud, but then it popped back as good as new? Occasionally though, someone would sit on one of those hats which was not the collapsible kind and mangle it all to flinders. The owner would pick it up, put it on his head and look extremely silly, eliciting guffaws of laughter from the audience. Those were the days. You don't see comedy like that anymore. They never sat on Dracula's hat, though--they wouldn't dare. But I digress. It's fun to digress.

Where was I? Oh yeah. Count Dracula was a vampire, one of the living dead who preyed on the living, much like lawyers and IRS agents. They sometimes outdo him, though, by getting blood out of a turnip.

160

People tried to dissuade Dracula from drinking blood and suggested he try tomato juice, but it gave him heartburn, and cranberry juice was too tart, so he stuck with blood. Many people tried wearing onions around their necks, thinking it was a sure-fire remedy to keep vampires away; in fact, it kept everybody away so that fad didn't last very long. Dracula knew that the real remedy was not onions, but garlic, which made him break out with terrible hives, but he sure wasn't going to tell anybody.

People were always trying to stab Dracula in the heart with a sharp stick because that's how you kill a vampire, and sometimes they came close to poking his eye out. He would yell, "Watch out, you almost poked me in the eye with that thing!" He had been traumatized when just a young vampire by being poked in the eye and was very sensitive to it. One day, while passing an old-folks home, he heard laughing and yelling over the fence. There was a hole in the fence with a sign reading, "Look in here for an extraordinary, unforgettable experience!" So he peered through the hole and somebody poked him in the eye with a stick. Then he heard more laughing and yelling. He never got over that experience and is not a friend of the elderly.

Because of that happening, Dracula never went out during the day, only at night when there are fewer people about. He would sleep all day in his coffin--I told you he was weird. Then, when the sun went down and the moon came over the mountain and Kate Smith started singing, he would jump out of his coffin and scare the living crap out of her. Once he scared her so badly, that her voice changed to a basso profundo. This actually worked to her advantage later on, though, when she was able to do the voice of Darth Vader in the *Star Wars* movies.

Count Dracula lived in Transylvania, somewhere near Saskatoon, in a dark, gloomy, worn down, spooky, old castle with bats flitting about. Speaking of bats, whenever Dracula found himself in a jam, he would turn into a bat and fly away. Now tell me, of all the creatures in the world, why would he choose to turn into a BAT!? They are the ugliest, most repulsive creatures on earth. Why didn't he choose a stately eagle, a beautiful peacock or even a pretty little parakeet? But ohh nooo, he wanted to be a bat. "Well, there's no accounting for taste," said the woman as she kissed the walrus.

Sometimes, Dracula would invite people over, but why they went is beyond me. He would welcome them with, "Vy good evenink and velcome to da house of Drakula!" (He spoke with an accent much like Bela Lugosi). "Let me take your hat and troat; I vood like to suck your blood!" Dracula was a card and often entertained at parties.

We all know that Count Dracula is living (?) on borrowed time. Someday, somebody is going to be successful with that sharp stick and poke him right through the heart, which will handicap him severely. In fact, it will disable him forever as long as the stake remains in his heart. But as soon as someone pulls it out, you better not be there 'cause he's really gonna be pissed!

THE MUMMY[6]

To me, the scariest of the famous monsters I have known is the Mummy. Not that cartoon character which Brendan Fraser has been chasing around in a more recent series of movies. I'm talking about the real, original Mummy with no special effects, just bandages. I spent many a Saturday afternoon crouched down low, peering between the theater seats whenever the Mummy came on the screen. Sometimes people would say to me, "Hand me a wad of gum while you're down there."

His rampage began when some clumsy archaeologist discovered his tomb in ancient Egypt and broke into it despite the dire warning which was carved on the door, "If you break into my tomb, you better watch out!" The Mummy's name was *Kharis,* and he had been buried alive 3,000 years ago because he *trifled* with the Pharaoh's daughter, Ananka.

Trifled is a polite way of saying what we all know really happened. In fact, they were quite the talk of Thebes back then, as evidenced by an inscription found within the tomb reading, "Kharis and Ananka sitting in a tree, K-i-s-s-i-n-g." Before being buried, Kharis' tongue was cut out by his accusers, after which he refused to ever speak to them again.

Then he was awakened after 3,000 years asleep and was really cranky because they had interrupted his nap. He was on a mission to catch all those who had defiled his tomb and just squeeze them silly. There was a complication though, because after being cramped in one position for 3,000 years, his left leg was asleep so he dragged his foot when he walked. Either that or he had stepped in camel poo and was trying to wipe it off. This made it extremely difficult to catch those he wanted to squeeze silly. They could easily outrun him and would taunt him by yelling, "Mummy, Mummy, you look like a dummy, and you can't even catch your own grandmummy!" This really teed him off, but he had a secret weapon. Having been shut up in his sarcophagus for 3,000 years, he had not been able to take a bath and was really ripe. So after locating his intended victims, he would wave his armpit at them making them pass out from the stench. Then he would grab them and squeeze them silly.

Like the other famous monsters I have known, the Mummy was indestructible. He was set on fire several times, had a building dropped on him and was drowned in a swamp, but he always returned in the sequel to continue his annoying habit of squeezing people silly.

THE WOLFMAN[7]

The Wolfman was a terrifying creature to behold with his hairy face, sharp claws, snarling mouth and fangs, looking much like Fidel Castro. Every time a full moon appeared, Lawrence Talbot (that was his real name) would turn into a werewolf. He had earlier been bitten by a werewolf, so naturally he turned into one. Go figure. Then he would go about ripping people's throats out which made them very angry--it ruined many a clean shirt.

However, it wasn't his fault because he warned people that he would turn into a monster and kill them. He even begged them to lock him up for the night, but they wouldn't listen. They would say, "Yea, yea, we'll believe that when we see it." Well they saw, and then it was too late. It was as if they hadn't been at rehearsal or seen the movies before, because it happened in so many of them. Even after the murder the next day, when he was back to normal, Larry would tell the police he had ripped the guy's throat out, but they would just snicker and say, "No, he nicked himself shaving."

The only thing that would stop a werewolf was a silver bullet, but they were not easy to come by. You had to make your own. People tried borrowing some from the Lone Ranger, but he was saving his to give to ranchers he had rescued who would say, "Who was that masked man?" as he and Tonto rode off into the sunset. Then the sheriff would look into the rancher's hand and say, "A silver bullet. Why, don't you know who that was? That was the Great Pumpkin!" And then you'd hear, "Hi-yo Silver, away!" as the William Tell Overture crescendoed. Ah, what drama! I loved it!

But back to our story. At the end of each Wolfman movie, someone would somehow come up with a silver bullet, and then just at the climactic moment when the Wolfman was about to pounce on him, he would fire the silver bullet, killing his attacker. Now the interesting thing about killing a werewolf is that after dying, he changes back into the person he originally was and people would say, "Why, it wasn't a werewolf after all, it was Herman Schmedly!"

In Lawrence Talbot's case, they said "What happened?" and his killer said, "I just killed a werewolf."

They said, "No you didn't, you killed Larry. Look!"

So he looked and sure enough, it was Larry.

Once again though, in the next movie Larry would come back to life and pretend that nothing had happened.

THE INVISIBLE MAN[8]

A rather amusing famous monster is the Invisible Man. Technically speaking, he is not a monster, but a human bean, but since he did such monstrous deeds, like causing death and destruction and not using a handkerchief when he sneezed, I include him here. I sometimes call him *IM* for short because he was not much taller than Claude Rains. His name was Griffin, who somehow discovered the secret to invisibility, and boy did he have fun! He would sneak into the girls' locker room and really enjoy himself. One of the girls would say, "Do you feel someone breathing," but another girl would say, "Oh no, that's just a draft coming through those holes that were bored through the wall from the boys' locker room."

The drug he took to make himself invisible eventually drove him around the bend, and he became as wacky as a campaigning politician. He began killing people by wrecking trains, blowing up buildings and not showering for a month, all those things that we all aspire to do someday.

Wherever there was a disaster in the world like a flood, earthquake or rock concert, people would say, "The Invisible Man did it!"

Others would say, "How do you know, did you see him do it?"

Then the accusers would nervously change the subject like, "Well, no, but...er...um my sister once knew a guy who could put nine golf balls in his mouth at the same time."

Occasionally, newspapers would publish IM's picture with a reward notice, but people couldn't see anything, so they went around with baseball bats swatting at empty space hoping to hit him, usually just hitting each other.

One guy tried to collect the reward by bringing in a big empty box and announcing, "I've caught the Invisible Man!"

The police said, "Prove it,"

So the person nudged the box with his foot to make it move and out of the corner of his mouth said, "Help, let me out, I'm the Invisible Man!" He didn't fool anybody though because the police saw his mouth move like a bad ventriloquist.

Ventriloquists today don't seem to care if their mouths do move. On TV they just blatantly talk away while moving their dummy's mouth and limbs. It looks ridiculous and is very off-putting. The most famous ventriloquist ever was Edgar Bergen whose mouth moved all the time, but since he was on the radio nobody could tell or even cared. The notion of a ventriloquist on the radio always seemed a bit odd to me though. If it weren't for the fact that Charlie McCarthy and Mortimer Snerd were real people, Bergen would never have made it in any other medium.

Of course the great advantage to being invisible is that you can sneak into any place you want. Just think, going to the mall, the library, the flea market, the possibilities are endless. The IM could be sitting beside you right now! Doesn't that make your spine tingle and your hair stand on end? Boo! Did I scare you? Why don't you take a baseball bat right now and try swatting the air beside you just in case. Go ahead, I won't tell anybody.

One way the police tried to catch the IM was to blow smoke about, but that just made everybody cough and choke so they had to stop that. The IM was a chain smoker, so it didn't bother him. They thought they would be able to see him when it rained, but he just raised an umbrella and floated away like Mary Poppins. They also looked for his tracks in the snow, but he used a pogo stick and they thought the tracks were being made by an invisible, one-legged kangaroo.

A problem for the IM was clothing. Of course, he couldn't wear any, so in cold weather he would shiver and sneeze a lot. People would say, "Gesundheit!" then look around, see no one and feel foolish. One day, while he was watching a group of boys daring each other to put their tongues on a frozen flagpole, his bare butt accidently touched the pole. His ensuing shriek could be heard all the way to the Dalai Lama. He tried to run away but was stuck and had to wait until the spring thaw to get loose because nobody knew he was stuck.

Eventually, his invisibility wore off, but he didn't realize it until he went outside with no clothes on. People began pointing and falling down with laughter. One little boy said, "Look Mommy, that man is all em-bare-assed." And he was. In fact, he was so humiliated, that he went away somewhere to sulk and was never seen again.

30 - MOBY FISH[9]

Call me Iggy Schpielman, bosun's mate on the good ship Lollipop. Thus begins the tale of Moby Fish, about the struggle of humanity vs. nature, the comprehensible vs. the inscrutable, man vs. fish, shorts vs. briefs. It explores the question, *Can a mariner from a small whaling town on the coast find happiness as the spouse of a wealthy and titled fishmonger...or whether 'tis nobler in the mind to bear the slings and arrows of outrageous fortune...or...uh...*Sorry...lost my train of thought...

Moby Fish is the story of the evil and scheming Captain Rehab and his zany pursuit of the great white whale, Moby Fish. When Rehab was just a juvenile delinquent, he owned a tiny little guppy which he kept in a fish bowl, but Rehab grew tired of taking care of it and flushed it down the toilet. This frightful experience was so traumatic for the little guppy that he turned from black to white. The guppy's name was Moby Fish.

Thinking that was the end of it, little Rehab went about his business of being incorrigible, not realizing that his little guppy had survived and was washed out to sea where it began to grow and grow and grow. This may have been due to his being washed out near a nuclear power plant which dumped its contaminated waste into the ocean. Eventually, Moby grew into a whale of a fish, the biggest anyone had ever seen, so people started calling him Moby Whale. Not only did the fish grow, but his resentment toward Rehab for flushing him down the toilet also grew at about the same intensity, and he vowed to get that little brat someday.

Moby Fish considered the ocean his personal playground and swam around wrecking sailing ships, swallowing people whole and later spitting them out just for fun. We know that whales do this from the story of Jonah and the whale in the Bible and Monstro the whale in Pinocchio. In the process, however, Moby couldn't resist biting off a few legs and things. He was mischievous but kinda cute for his size...and he was looking for Rehab.

Over the years, Rehab also grew up and developed a love and fascination for whaling. Boy, nothing was more thrilling to him than hurling a huge harpoon to snag a fleeing whale then watching the blood gush out. Almost as exciting was lashing it to the side of the ship where it could be torn apart to use for many of the necessities of life, like oil for our lamps and perfume to make the ladies smell purty. The oil comes from the blubber of the whale, and the perfume is made from the ambergris, whatever that is. Have you ever been on an elevator when a lady enters wearing way too much ambergris? On several occasions I've come near barfing. I'd rather smell the dead whale!

One day, while chasing a particularly large, white whale, Rehab recognized it as his very own guppy, Moby Fish, for he was still wearing his store label, "Al's Pet Emporium 39 cts." (Yes, some pet stores used to label their fish.) Just as Rehab was about to unleash his harpoon, the whale suddenly turned and rammed the ship sending everyone on board into the water. Moby Fish proceeded to gobble up a few of the seamen and then recognized Rehab. As the whale turned toward him, spooky music was heard, and a great white shark swam between them. The whale said to the shark in fish talk, "Get outta here, dummy! You're in the wrong movie." The shark replied, "Oh! Sorry. I heard the music and couldn't resist." When the music reached a crescendo and Rehab was just scrambling back aboard ship, Moby Fish latched onto his leg, biting it clean off.

Well, Rehab was laid up for quite a while stewing and burning up with vengeance, swearing he would get even. "I hate that stupid whale!" was all he could say. As a bit of irony, he had a new leg made out of a sperm whale's jaw bone, thus making another whale mad at him. Thereafter, Rehab clunked when he walked about.

Eventually, Rehab was given his own whaling ship to command: the Peepot. But every time he took his ship out, the incensed Captain Rehab was constantly looking for the white whale that had taken his leg. With every passing ship, Rehab would hail the captain and yell, "Have you seen a big white whale?"

Usually, the answer was negative, "No, but I once saw a blue hippopotamus wearing pants after an all-night grog at the Belching Parrot Pub," and then laughter. Rehab met such derision calmly under his breath, "Wise guy," and tossed a harpoon after him.

He once met Captain Hook and asked him the same question. Hook replied, "All I've seen is some annoying little fairy in green tights who keeps following me around, demanding that I give him his *tinkle bell!*" He then saluted Rehab with his hooked hand and nearly knocked himself out.

Captain Queeg responded to the same query by asking, "Have you seen the missing strawberries?"

Captain Nemo tried to ram the Peepot, and Captain Bligh vowed, "I'll hang him from the highest yardarm in the British fleet!"

Rehab remarked to his crew, "There sure are a lot of nutty sea captains out here." The crew just rolled their eyes and looked away.

Captain Rehab was so obsessed with his vengeance that he nailed a gold doubloon to the main mast and said to his crew, "This goes to the first man who spots me that white whale!" Well, this got everybody so excited they started break dancing right there. Nobody wanted the doubloon—-it had a hole in it, but everybody wanted that mast. You could build a whole ship around it. What is a doubloon anyway, some kind of bird?

A few of the crewmen got together and planned to get the reward through subterfuge. Some of them didn't know what that meant but went along just to be in the clique. They got a huge, hot-air balloon shaped like a whale from the Thanksgiving Parade and painted it white. Then they put it in the water and had the lookout yell, "Thar she blows!" which means, "I see a whale over thar!" Captain Rehab saw the faux white whale, immediately grabbed his harpoon and chucked it as hard as he could at the balloon. The resulting explosion nearly blew the Peepot out of the water and sent Rehab sprawling on his back. When he recovered his senses, he glared from under his low, dark eyebrows and growled, "I hate that stupid whale!"

Captain Rehab's first mate was named *Starbuck* who was responsible for making coffee in the morning for which he charged everyone six bucks a cup. He would later open a franchise in his name and make a fortune. He was inspired by Rusty Drainpipe, the first person to ever put water in a bottle and sell it to a gullible public. Rusty used words like *crystal clear, mountain pure* and *fresh as a newly-brushed mouth* to advertise his bottled water. Other bottlers followed and claimed that their water cured dropsy, consumption, leprosy and warts, but it all came right out of the same kitchen sink, proving that people will buy anything if it's cleverly promoted. Just like this book. Some would call it *creative marketing.*

It was Starbuck who always tried to calm Rehab whenever he got excited about the white whale, which was quite often. Whenever the lookout yelled, "Thar she blows!" Rehab would clunk to the rail and strain to see the color.

He would yell, "Is it white!?"

Usually the answer came back, "No, just grey," or "blue" or "pink."

Then Rehab would clunk about ranting and raving, "Oooh! Dirty rackin' fratcher!" And when Starbuck stepped in to calm him, Rehab would yell, "Avast there, Coffee Breath!" (I think that means, *Shut up!*) "I hate that stupid whale!"

Other crew members were *Stubb,* so called because he also had something bitten off, *Elmo,* the pyromaniac who repeatedly tried to set the ship on fire, and Iggy Schpielman's special South Pacific friend, Quickquack or Quatzlcoatl or Chungookchuck, or something like that. He had grown up a cannibal, so Iggy promptly turned down all his dinner invitations and wouldn't let Quickquack stand behind him.

He was a particularly dreary fellow who was always predicting death and doom for the Peepot. On one occasion, after foreseeing his own death in his Magic 8 Ball which he used for fortune telling, Quickquack gave all his possessions to Iggy, ordered his own water-tight coffin built and went into an impenetrable trance. No one could rouse him from it. They tried by stabbing him in the eye with their Swiss army knives, slamming his hand in a car door and hitting him in the face with a baseball bat, but nothing elicited the slightest reaction from him.

Until one day, when the call came, "Thar she blows!"

A wild-eyed Captain Rehab shouted, "What color?"

And the answer returned, "White!"

Well, Quickquack and the whole crew suddenly went nuts. At once, it seemed they were all caught up in Captain Rehab's feverish frenzy, grabbing harpoons and knocking each other over in a rush to launch the longboats. They were halfway to the whale when they heard the cry, "Wait, come back!" They had forgotten Rehab who had stopped to go potty.

After retrieving him and scolding, "See what happens when you dilly-dally," they set out again with even greater gusto.

The crew began throwing their harpoons with no effect until Rehab shouted, "Stop! You're wasting ammunition!"

Then Starbuck suggested, "Captain, this'll never work. Let's go back, get the submarine and put a torpedo up his--"

Rehab interrupted, "The last time we tried that, Moby Fish thought the sub was another whale and tried to mate with it. Many of the crew are still in counseling from that experience." So they continued onward.

Moby Fish saw them coming and decided to toy with them, so he flicked his fluke each time a longboat drew near, upending it with all hands. Then he said to himself, "I'll fix these guys," and dove as deeply as he could. Above him, the surging sea grew deathly calm, save the quiet sound of the gentle waves lapping lightly against the gunwales. (Those are the sides of the boats. Pause here to appreciate the poetic imagery.)

The crew feared that at any moment the whale would breach (that means come to the top), but they didn't know when. Captain Rehab, being the most experienced among them shouted, "Watch the birds! Watch the birds!" With that, a huge flock of laughing sea gulls gathered above and pooped all over the crew.

Rehab said, "I told you to watch the birds! Good thing whales can't fly! Ha! Ha! Ha!" Captain Rehab had his jocular side, though the crew failed to appreciate it.

Suddenly, to everyone's surprise, in the wink of an eye, without warning or a moment's notice, in a split second and out of the clear blue sky...er...water, Moby Fish came crashing through the surface. Straight up out of the sea he rose like a Saturn rocket, soaring high above, then avalanching downward right on top of them. After the wreckage cleared, there was Iggy Schpielman floating alone in the water. All the others had been drownded except Rehab.

Swimming off toward the horizon was the white whale, and astride his back, riding him like the wild bull at the Sitngulp Saloon, was Captain Rehab shouting at the top of his voice, "I hate this stupid whale!!!"

Iggy lay back in the water realizing that he probably would not survive when Quickquack's water-tight coffin suddenly burst to the surface with such force that it killed him instantly. *And the great shroud of the sea rolled on as it rolled five thousand years ago.*

31 – ONCE UPON A TIME

Now that we've been to the movies, a two-dimensional medium, I'd like to conclude with a discussion of the fourth dimension: *time*. (I'm gonna skip 3D because people in those funny-lookin' glasses scare me.) We refer to time...all the time: time heals all wounds, time is up, there's no time like the present, time and tide wait for no man, time marches on, Rudy Vallee sang, "My time is your time." Many of us have time on our hands, and some people even serve time. But what is time; what does it look like? Someone once said, "Time flies," so it must have wings like a bird. Someone else said, "Time is short," so it must resemble Danny DeVito. We even have a hint of its color and texture from the expression *time is money*. So time must be a short, green, wrinkled, thing with wings. However, no one has ever SEEN time.

Time also passes and stands still. We take time, we spend time, we waste time, we mark time. We also measure time...time and time again. How can we measure something that we've never seen? Nevertheless, we have watches, clocks, sundials, hour glasses and calendars, all of which measure time. We measure it in units of seconds, minutes, hours, days, weeks, months, years, decades, centuries, millennia, ages and eons. We even have moments, split seconds, jiffies, shakes of lambs' tails, in the wink of an eye, back in a flash and *right after this message.* For the sports enthusiast, there are periods, quarters and halves. In music there is 3/4 time, 4/4 time, etc. We have *tea* time, *tee* time and free time. There used to be a *Howdy Doody Time.* Where did we get all this time?

Once upon a time, there must have been a time when there was no time, if you catch my drift. Way back before there was anything, just space, time couldn't have passed because nothing was happening. There was no need for time, so there was none.

I'm sure there was God and maybe some angels sitting around.

Then one of the angels must have said, "This is boring--nothing's happening."

Another one said, "I know; let's go bowling."

A third said, "But we have nothing to bowl with."

And that's why God created the Universe. Our solar system is a big bowling alley and the planets are the balls they used!

After a while, they all got tired of bowling and said, "Now what'll we do?"

The first angel said, "Turn on the TV."

But another one said, "We don't have a TV; it hasn't been invented yet. Let's go up and see what God's doing."

They found God in his thinking chair, and He told them, "I've been creating *time*, so everyone will have something to do. From now on, everyone will have to keep track of time, be on time, take time, spend time and save time."

The angel Raphael asked, "How did you come up with this idea?"

God answered, "Well, I was just biding my time, when I came up with the idea of creating a whole lot of time so we can spend the time measuring everything we do. So far, I've created about four and a half billion years."

Then the angel Gabriel said, "But you've created so much time, we'll never be able to use it all!"

The angel Michael suggested, "Why don't you create someone to help us spend all this time."

Raphael offered, "How do you know those you create will be smart enough to use the time wisely and not squander it?"

Michael said, "If they ever have trouble, we can go down and help them out from time to time."

God approved, "That's a good idea, Mike. Then that will give you guys something to do, too. All the angels will be guardians and messengers."

Raphael was hesitant, "As for me, I'd rather just stay here and paint. Look at my latest painting. It's a Ninja Turtle."

Gabriel asked, "What's a *Ninja Turtle?*"

Raphael tried to explain, "I'm not sure, but the name seems to be calling me."

Gabriel commented, "Well, anybody can paint by numbers. Besides, I'd rather play the trumpet."

Raphael returned, "Oh, you're always blowing your own horn!"

God's mind was made up, so he created a race of humans, placed them on the planet earth and gave them all the time in the world to live and to govern themselves. They had free will and could do anything they wanted with their time as long as they followed the Golden Rule.

Gabriel asked, "What's the Golden Rule?"

Raphael told him, "That's the one where you do unto others before they do unto you."

God corrected him, "No, Raphael, it's *do unto others as you would have them do unto you.*."

Raphael responded, "Oh, sorry, I knew it was something like that."

Michael asked, "What are you going to call this race of human beings?"

God answered, "I'm going to call it *Man.*"

Michael said, "Oh, cool. He looks just like you."

THE CAVE MEN DISCOVER TIME

So Man began his existence on earth for the purpose of using all the time God had created. It was rough going at first. Man didn't know how he was supposed to use all the time he had been given. Then the cave men began some serious thinking.

Grunk said to Org, "That big orange thing came up in the sky again this morning."

Org answered, "Yeah, I know, and that big white thing was there in the night sky, but it looked like someone had taken a big bite out of it. I wonder what it all means."

Grunk responded, "Since it happens every day and every night, maybe we're supposed to count every time it happens."

Org agreed, "Okay, but to make it easier, we should have names for these things."

Grunk was curious, "You're right. What're we gonna call 'em?"

Org suggested, "Well, since the big orange thing comes out only when it's bright and sunny, why don't we call it the *sun*?

Grunk agreed and asked, "How 'bout that big white thing?"

Org had an answer for that, too, "I've been thinking about it, and you know when that hostile tribe comes over the hill, drops their loin cloths and moons us? Well, it reminds me of the big white thing, so why don't we call it the *moon*?"

Grunk was excited, "Great idea! We can make up some bumper stickers!"

Then Org observed, "I've also noticed that about every thirty nights a new moon appears, it gets bigger and bigger night after night until it's as big as a pizza, then it gets smaller and smaller and eventually disappears. Suddenly, it comes back and does the same thing all over again. I'm thinking we should count every time it does this as one moon."

Grunk, "Check!"

So the cave men had named the sun and the moon and started counting days, nights and months. Time had begun.

Then they noticed that about every twelve moons, the same things would happen over and over again. First, IT would warm up, flowers would begin blooming and the Easter Bunny would come. Next IT would get very, very hot, people would go to the beach and Disney World and the Yankees would win the pennant. After that, IT would cool off, the leaves would fall off the trees and men would watch football. Then IT would get very cold and snow, they would have to put chains on their sledges and Sandy Claws would show up. The cave men never figured out what *IT* was, but they knew that these cycles were significant and should be counted every time they start over. So they were then counting years.

After a while, Org grew concerned. He asked Grunk, "What year is this?"

Grunk told him, "Three."

Org said, "I'm getting very confused trying to keep track of all this time that's passing. I can't tell one day from another. We need to name the days."

Grunk wondered, "Well, what're we gonna call 'em?

Org responded, "Let's see. We should call the first day we saw the sun, *Sun Day*. We saw the moon that night, so let's call the next day, *Moon Day*. By the next day, we will have had two days and two nights, so let's call it, *Twos Day*. My daughter wants to get married the following day, so I want to name that day, *The day my daughter wants to get married day*."

Grunk suggested, "That's an awful long name. Why don't we just shorten it to *Wed Day*?"

Org said, "That's good. Then the next day is when we all go down to the river and fill our water skins and canteens, so why don't we call it, *Thirst Day*? And the next day is when we get together for our weekly pterodactyl fry, so let's call it, *Fry Day*."

Grunk offered, "Yeah, and remember after we had done all that stuff, not to mention hunting dinosaur and dragging women around by the hair, we were so tired we just sat around all day. So we should call that one *Sat Day.*"

Org added, "Since we experience that tiredness every seven days, why don't we call every seven-day period a weak, because that's how we feel. We'll change the spelling so there's no confusion."

Grunk was happy, "Yay!"

Org was still concerned, "You know, that's all fine, but it's still gonna be very confusing to remember it all. We need a big chart on which we can record all the days, weeks and moons."

Grunk was puzzled, "Well, what are we gonna call that?"

Org answered, "We can call it a *colander.*"

Grunk said, "That's something my wife uses to drain the spaghetti."

"Oh, right." Org thought for a moment, "Okay, we can change it to *calendar.*"

"Where we gonna keep this *calendar*?" Grunk wondered.

"We can draw it on the wall of your cave," Org suggested.

Grunk protested, "Oh no! My wife's mad at me already for drawing animals all over the walls. "

"Then let's put it in Blech's cave. He's not married, so he won't mind."

After they had drawn the calendar on Blech's wall, they drew a picture of a pretty girl for each month, since Blech was a playboy. Then they stood back to admire it.

Blech observed, "Those girls sure are purty, but you never meet girls who look like that in real life." Then he said, "Y'all named the days of the week, fellas, but'cha ain't named the moons. Dont'cha wanna call them somethin'? " (Blech was from Mississippi.)

Grunk and Org stared blankly at each other.

Blech continued, "If it don't make no never mind to y'all, we could just leave that up to Julius Caesar when he comes along"

They shook hands all around.

When everybody heard of the new calendar, they all went to Blech's cave to see it. However, the cave got too crowded, and everyone expected Blech to serve cocktails and hors d'oeuvre, so he told them to go draw a calendar in their own caves, which they did. Then everyone could tell which day of the week it was, and they could keep track of birthdays, holidays and dental appointments.

Some people began to wonder what they would do when the calendar runs out. After some discussion, they decided that they would start a new calendar, and to announce to everyone that a new year had begun, they would drop a big rock off of their only skyscraper, the two-story New Year Square Building, in the middle of the last night of the year. They rigged it so that when the rock hit the ground, the year *4* would light up. If they didn't see it, everybody should be able to hear it. Everyone got so excited that they all crowded tightly together in New Year Square, to tie up traffic, pick pockets and do the Macarena. They shouted, "Let's party hearty until the wee hours of the morning, wake up with booming headaches and have to call in sick to work!"

The president of the cave men, Rocky O'Bama (he was Irish), said, "Since we know everyone will be sick that day, why don't we all just take the day off, stay home and watch football. I proclaim it a legal holiday: *Hangover Day.*"

Everyone was jubilant, "Hurrah!" but some people said, "Yeah, but he wouldn't have done that if it weren't an election year."

Looking back over the year, Grunk was very satisfied, "Wow! We really accomplished a lot! We ought to name this creative process." He pondered a moment. Suddenly a light bulb appeared over his head, and he exclaimed to Org, "I know! We can name it after you, since it was your idea! We can call it getting *ORGanized*!"

Org blushed and shuffled his feet, "Aw shucks!"

GO OUTSIDE,
AND SEE WHAT TIME IT IS

Many thousands of Hangover Days later, the Ancient Egyptians began experimenting with methods of keeping time. They also had a calendar with days and moons on it, but they measured not only the days, they began measuring the hours within the day.

Pharaoh Hotntot had an adviser named Tic Toc who one day stuck a stick in the ground and said to his Pharaoh, "Look, Phary, when I stick this stick in the ground it makes a shadow which moves around it in a circle."

Hotntot said, "So what?"

Tic Toc replied, "Well, by following this shadow we can measure the hours of the day. We can make marks on the ground, and when the shadow reaches a certain mark, that's what time it is."

Pharaoh was unimpressed, "What good will that do?"

"Well, then we will know what time to eat," Tic Toc explained.

Pharaoh stated, "I already know what time to eat...when I get hungry."

Still, Tic Toc persisted, "You can also use it to tell when your favorite TV shows come on."

Pharaoh looked perplexed, "What's a TV show?"

Tic Toc was embarrassed, "Oh right, I forgot, it hasn't been invented yet."

In a final effort to impress Pharaoh, Tic Toc stuck the stick on a table and drew the hours around it. Then he took it into the palace to show Pharaoh, but to Tic Toc's horror, the shadow had disappeared. So he went back outside again and discovered that the shadow was back. He concluded that his invention would only work outside. He later found out that it would not work at night. Also, it proved impractical as a wrist watch.

Pharaoh Hotntot was not pleased with this monumental waste of time, so he ordered Tic Toc to be mummified. Tic Toc pleaded that his only interest was in trying to please Pharaoh, and that he shouldn't be punished for making one mistake.

Hotntot explained, "I'm not punishing you for failing, I'm executing you for calling me *Phary.*"

Tic Toc never knew what a wonderful invention he had created, but his name lives on today in mechanical clocks around the world: *Tic-Toc, Tic-Toc, Tic-Toc.*

JULIE'S CALENDAR

Then one day in 45 B.C., just as Blech had forseen, Julius Caesar arrived, saw the calendar and asked, "Quo feminae pectore humungos?" which is Latin for, "Where are the Dallas Cowboy Cheerleaders?" By the time Julie saw the calendar, many alterations had been made to it. After all, thousands of years had passed since the cave men first created it.

The most significant change was that every influential person who had encountered the calendar over the years named a month after him or herself. For example, it had months named after Nebuchadnezzar, Attila the Hun, Orson Welles, Mickey Mouse, Helen of Troy, General Patton, Socrates, Alexander the Great, Melvin the Mediocre, Cleopatra, Barney Rubble and Salma Hayek. In all, there were 147 months in the calendar year. Well, this was too much for Caesar, so he proclaimed, "Ima gotta colda caboosa!" which means, "I feel a draft under my toga!" He then said, "From now on, there will be only twelve months, and no month will be named after anybody...except me!" And that's why today we have the month of *Julie*.

Julius Caesar named the other months as well, including the month of March, which is helpful to us because we all know what happened on March 15, 44 B.C. Without Julie's calendar, we wouldn't know when it happened.

THE POPE'S LEAP YEAR CALENDAR

Now we come to the calendar which we still use today. It is called the *Gregorian Calendar* and was introduced to the world in 1582 by Pope Gregory XIII. The reason the Gregorian Calendar was developed is that the old Julian Calendar was based on a year of 360 days, but it actually takes the Earth $365\frac{1}{4}$ days to orbit the sun. So under the old calendar, before they knew it, they were celebrating Christmas in the middle of summer. Of course, to people in Australia, this is perfectly normal, but that's another story.

After years of research, the Pope's astronomers determined that the calendar was out of date. So they said, "Hey Pope, we need a new calendar."

When he asked, "Why?" they replied, "Because we haven't done our Christmas shopping yet, so we need to move Christmas back to winter when most of the stores have their Christmas sales."

The Pope asked, "How are we gonna do that?"

The astronomers answered, "We'll have to drop ten days from the year in order to catch up."

The Pope said okay, so ten days were dropped from the month of October in 1582. What would have been Friday, October 5, became Friday, October 15. The new calendar was first adopted only in Italy, Poland, Portugal and Spain. So if you are Italian, Polish, Portuguese or Spanish and were born during this ten-day period, you do not exist!

People in Great Britain and America were so confused by the new calendar that they resisted adopting it until 1752, but by that time, the Julian Calendar had become even further outdated. It was then necessary to drop eleven days from the calendar, so in 1752, during the month of September, eleven days were dropped. Thursday, September 3, became Thursday, September 14, thus eliminating a bunch more people who were born during those eleven days.

Even though the Gregorian Calendar was a great improvement over the Julian Calendar, that one-quarter extra day that it takes the Earth to revolve around the sun means that every four years we lose a day.

The Pope, being a very astute observer of events around him exclaimed, "That's gonna screw everything up! What are we gonna do about it?"

The astronomers calmed him, "Don't worry about it, Your Popeness. We'll just add an extra day to the month of February every four years, then everything will come out even."

The Pope was so pleased that he leaped for joy. You've probably never seen a pope leap. That's why every fourth year is called *Leap Year*.

They even created a mnemonic (a memory jogger) to help us remember this irregularity in the calendar, and I quote, "Thirty days hath September, April, June and November. All the rest have thirty-one, except February which is weird and has only twenty-eight days but gets an extra day added to it every four years, unless the year is divisible by 100, except when it's divisible by 400..." Got that?

THE END OF THE WORLD

No discussion of time and the measurement thereof would be complete without including the Maya, a civilization which lived in Mexico and Central America way back before anybody can remember, except maybe Shirley MacLaine in her former life. They made a calendar which started on August 13, 3114 B.C. The reason we can be so precise about the date is that in 1967, a man emerged from the Central American jungle and announced that he was a Mayan who had been abducted by an alien spaceship. He said that the aliens had actually created the Mayan calendar just to confuse everybody and to put them all in a *tizzy* (an alien word meaning, *Where the heck are my car keys--and more importantly, where the heck is my car?!*)

They also told him that they had nothing to do with the Nazca Lines in Peru, the Pyramids, the Easter Island faces, crop circles or any other phenomena of which they have been accused. They asked him to tell everyone that if we don't cease and desist in such slanderous accusations, they will take legal action or blow us all to bits, whichever mood strikes them first.

As you probably know, the Mayan calendar has become infamous for its prediction that the end of the world would occur on December 21, 2012, or so some people believe. On the other hand, some scholars say that it does no such thing, that it merely predicts the coming of a new age on that date. But that's such a boring theory that most people would rather believe the end-of-the-world scenario. So, as this book goes to press, the end of the world may be looming. If you purchased this book before December 21, you'd better read it in a hurry, and I wouldn't worry about doing any Christmas shopping this year. However, if you're reading it after that date and are still here, then you're probably safe and can assume that the Maya were full of crap. Either that, or you're still using an outdated Julian Calendar.

HAPPY NEW MILLENNIUM!

One question which the calendar makers have never made clear to people is, "On which date do we convert from one millennium to another?" Remember back in 1999 when we were approaching the year 2000? Many people believed that the shift in time was going to cause catastrophic events around the world: computers were going to crash, airliners would fall from the sky, Ronald McDonald would suffer fallen arches, Vanna White would forget how to spell. How relieved we all were when the time came and passed and nothing unfortunate happened, except the six billionth person was born into the world. His first words were, "Move over!"

This change in date was so confusing that many people believed that the new millennium would begin on January 1, 2000, when actually it didn't begin until January 1, 2001. A simple test of proof is to count up to ten. You always begin with *one*, and you always include the *ten*. Therefore, when counting to 2,000 years, you must begin with the year *one* (there was no year *zero*) and if you don't pass out first, include the year *2,000*. Thus the new millennium began with the year 2,001. I hope everyone is satisfied with this explanation and will have no trouble when the year 3,000 rolls around. You're welcome.

We must now conclude our study of the origin, development and measurement of time. It is proper that mankind has always devoted so much time and effort to this topic since time is the force that frames our existence, that shapes our purpose, that makes life real. Either that or it's a meaningless and wasteful flight of fancy with absolutely no relevance whatsoever.

Well, I'd love to stay and continue sharing, but I've got to go. It's time now for my nap, and they're very strict about nap time around here.

ENDNOTES (Continued on next page)

1. (p. 57) The conversation between Nate and MAL was suggested by the one between Dave and H.A.L. in the 1968 MGM film, *2001: A Space Odyssey,* produced and directed by Stanley Kubrick and co-written by Kubrick and Arthur C. Clarke.

2. (P. 60) *"Crocodile" Dundee,* a 1986 film from Paramount Pictures, directed by Peter Faiman with screenplay by John Cornell, Paul Hogan and Ken Shadie.

3. (P. 91) Includes allusions to *The Wonderful Wizard of Oz* by L. Frank Baum, published in 1900, the basis for the 1939 MGM classic film, *The Wizard of Oz,* directed by Victor Fleming, et.al., with screenplay by Noel Langley, et.al.

4. (P. 157) *Frankenstein or The Modern Prometheus* is a novel written by Mary Shelley and first published anonymously in 1818. There are numerous film adaptations including the Universal Studios release in 1931 directed by James Whale and adapted from the Peggy Webling play by John L. Balderston. The screenplay was written by Francis Edward Faragoh and Garrett Fort with contributions from Robert Florey and John Russell. The character which came to be called *the Frankenstein monster* also appeared in *Bride of Frankenstein* (1935), *Son of Frankenstein* (1939), *Ghost of Frankenstein* (1942) and the four films listed under Endnote 7 below.

5. (P. 160) The 1897 novel, *Dracula,* by Bram Stoker has been adapted for film numerous times. The Universal Studios version in 1931 is based on the stage play by Hamilton Deane and John L. Balderston and was directed by Tod Browning with screenplay by Garrett Fort.

6. (P. 163) *The Mummy* is originally a 1932 film released by Universal Studios, written by John L. Balderston and directed by Karl Freund. In this version, the Mummy is a resurrected priest named *Imhotep*, and his love interest is the Princess Ankh-es-en-amun. In the four Universal sequels from the 1940's, listed below, the Mummy is named *Kharis*, and his princess is *Ananka:*

	Director	Writers
The Mummy's Hand (1940)	Christy Cabanne	Griffin Jay and Maxwell Shane
The Mummy's Tomb (1942)	Harold Young	Neil P. Varnick
The Mummy's Ghost (1944)	Reginald LeBorg	Griffin Jay and Henry Sucher
The Mummy's Curse (1944)	Leslie Goodwin	Leon Abrams and Dwight V.Babcock

ENDNOTES (Concluded)

7. (P. 165) *The Wolfman* from Universal Studios in 1941 was written by Curt Siodmak and directed by George Waggner. The Wolfman role was reprised by Universal in the following four films:

	Director
Frankenstein Meets the Wolfman (1943) Written by Curt Siodmak	Roy William Neill

House of Frankenstein (1944)
  Written by Edward T. Lowe, Jr.,
    and Curt Siodmak
	Earl C. Hinton

House of Dracula (1945) Written by Edward T. Lowe, Jr.	Earl C. Hinton

Abbott & Costello Meet Frankenstein (1948)
  Written by Robert Lees,
    Frederic I. Renaldo and John Grant
	Charles Barton

8. (P. 167) *The Invisible Man* is a novel written by H. G. Wells in 1897. The 1933 film adaptation from Universal Studios was directed by James Whale with a screenplay by R. C. Sheriff, Philip Wylie and Preston Sturges. There have been a number of sequels and spinoffs beginning with *The Invisible Man Returns* in 1940, directed by Joe May and written by Joe May, Curt Siodmak and Lester Cole. The other sequels are largely unrelated to the novel.

9. (P. 171) *Moby Fish* is based loosely on the 1851 novel, *Moby Dick*, by Herman Melville which was used for several film adaptations, most notably, the 1956 United Artists version directed by John Huston with screenplay by Ray Bradbury.